Benedita da Silva

An Afro-Brazilian Woman's Story of Politics and Love

Medea Benjamin & Maisa Mendonça

A PROJECT OF GLOBAL EXCHANGE

∼

FOOD FIRST BOOKS

OAKLAND, CALIFORNIA

BOOK DESIGN AND TYPESETTING BY HARVEST GRAPHICS
COVER DESIGN BY LORY POULSON
COVER PHOTO BY ANTÔNIO GUERREIRO

Library of Congress Cataloging-in-Publication Data

Silva, Benedita da.
    Benedita da Silva: an Afro-Brazilian woman's story of politics and
love / as told to Medea Benjamin and Maisa Mendonça.
        132 p.   22 cm.
    "A Food First book"
    ISBN 0-935028-70-6
    1. Silva, Benedita da. 2. Women legislators—Brazil—Biography. 3.
Women, Black—Brazil—Rio de Janeiro—Biography. 4. Women
political activists—Brazil—Rio de Janeiro—Biography. 5. Brazil—
Politics and government—1985- 6. Brazil—Social conditions—1985-
I. Benjamin, Medea, 1952- . II. Mendonça, Maisa, 1962- . III. Title.
F2538.5.S55A3 1997
328.981'092
[B]—DC21   97-22158
                                                                      CIP

Food First Books are distributed by:
    CDS
    425 Madison Avenue
    New York, NY 10017
    (800) 343-4499
    www.cdsbooks.com

FIFTH PRINTING

PRINTED IN USA

Photo by Rick Reinhard

Contents

Foreword

by Reverend Jesse Jackson

For a number of years, human rights activists here in the USA have been aware of and followed with interest the varied activities of Senator Benedita da Silva. Now she has given us this autobiographical record of the highlights of her life experiences, tragedy and triumph, sorrows and successes.

In these pages we learn about the everyday life among the urban poor of Brazil who, as in our country, number in the millions. The *favelas* of Brazil are the ghettos and barrios of the USA. In both countries, it is the children who suffer the most. Benedita knows this all too well, as her own childhood was marked by extreme poverty.

The book's straightforward, eloquent narrative reveals to us an admirable strength of character and a passionate commitment to the struggle against racism, sexism, and economic exploitation. In some way, the mission of relevant leadership is to disturb the comfortable in order to promote social change. Benedita has done just that. As a working-class organizer, feminist, parliamentarian, and defender of street children, Benedita da Silva has taken on formidable powers and forced them to change course. And like so many of our activists in the civil rights movement, Benedita's strength and fortitude is firmly anchored in a faith-based vision of her community.

Senator da Silva, as an Afro-Brazilian, is a member of the largest community of people of African heritage in our hemisphere. Slavery, racism and colonialism produced the odious western trade in human cargo and resulted in our community being uprooted and scattered all over the earth—from Rio and Port au Prince to Savannah and New York. Where our African ancestors were dropped off was merely a matter of a boat stop. Benedita's success in overcoming tremendous obstacles is therefore a success that our entire community should celebrate. And the realization of her dream will open the way for others to fulfill dreams of their own.

On a recent visit to Brazil, I had the opportunity to spend an afternoon visiting with Benedita and some of her neighbors at her house in the Chapéu Mangueira *favela* in Rio de Janeiro. It was a joyous occasion, which I and our Rainbow delegation will long remember with appreciation.

This autobiography is a publishing event of great importance. It is my fervent hope that this American edition will be widely read and discussed in every part of our country. It can open up avenues of international understanding and friendship that will help keep hope alive.

Rev. Jesse D. Jackson, Sr.

Founder and President, National Rainbow Coalition

Preface

My life is replicated in the lives of the many Beneditas, Marias, and Terezas that I represent: poor black women from the *favelas,* the slums. I live in a country of 30 million impoverished people, people who can't read and write, people who live in cardboard shacks in the shantytowns, under bridges, on the streets. I know their stories, because I have lived it myself.

I've been through many desperate times in my life. I saw my first child buried like a pauper. The image of my baby inside that little box will always be etched in my memory. I have a spiritual understanding of death, but that death was a violent one. I saw the precious baby I carried in my womb die, and I didn't have the means to bury him with dignity. I've been to the bottom of the well of despair and I know that unless you have something to keep you strong, you can go crazy or kill yourself. I was lucky to have a family who supported me and gave me the strength to survive.

I want this book to not only convey the sad times I've lived through, but to also portray the story of a champion—a champion who is not alone, who doesn't keep the trophy for herself. My trophy is shared with all those who are poor, discriminated against, dispossessed, down and out. They are the ones who inspire me.

I had hoped that this book would be written by a woman who had, like me, experienced what it is like to be discriminated against because of her social class or the color of her skin. I wanted it to be written by a black woman who could identify with what I have been through. This dream did not come true because my dear friend Lélia Gonzalez, who was planning to write my life story, is no longer with us. Even after her death, Lélia continues to be a great inspiration to me. That is why I want to dedicate this book to her.

When Maisa and Medea approached me to write a book and produce a video about my life, I was hesitant. I am a very private person and I couldn't imagine exposing my inner thoughts to people I hardly knew. But this time I had just returned from the Fourth International Women's Conference in Beijing, and I was moved by the opportunity to exchange experiences with so many wonderful women. I realized that this book could help me communicate with women around the world and perhaps even inspire other women who don't have the privilege of having someone record their life story.

I want to thank Maisa and Medea for making this project possible. We laughed together, we cried together, we talked about everything from my private life to my political dreams.

I also want to thank the readers for taking an interest in my life. You, too, may be of different races and classes, but I'm certain we share some of the same hopes and dreams for a better world. It would be wonderful if my story could give you just a bit more courage and strength to help build that world.

Acknowledgments

In Brazil, we are indebted to Bené's family for welcoming us into their lives: her husband Councilman Antônio Pitanga, her daughter Nilcea da Silva and her son Pedro Paulo da Silva. Bené's staff and advisors helped squeeze us into her jam-packed schedule and allowed us to comb through their archives. Special thanks to Cicera Moraes, Zulmira Pereira da Silva and Cleonice dos Santos in Brasília; and in Rio, Val Carvalho, Neilda Fabiano dos Santos, Mozart Porto Rangel, Ana Paula Costa, Jaime Muniz Martins, Antônio Galuzzio, Sandra Martins, Mauro Alemão, Everaldo Pereira and Ezequiel dos Santos. We also want to thank journalist Dulce Maria Pereira and Nani Stuart, the Workers Party Foreign Relations Advisor, for helping us make the first contact with Bené. For the Portuguese edition, we are thankful to Isabel Mauad, from Mauad Publishers in Rio.

Our whirlwind schedule while taping the interviews in Brazil would have been impossible without the unfailing support of Maisa's family in Rio: her mother Suely, her sister Luciana, and her grandmothers Margot and Ana. We owe an eternal debt to Medea's wonderful husband Kevin Danaher and children, Arlen and Maya, for putting up with all the late evening and weekend sessions while we sandwiched the book between full-time work.

In the U.S., we are ever grateful to the staff and board of Global Exchange for their enthusiastic support, particularly Co-Director Kirsten Moller, Rodrigo Gonzales and Jennifer Cariño for useful feedback, Elizabeth Wilcox and Lisa Russ for fundraising assistance, Tony Newman for his public relations work, and interns Jennifer Sanders, Megan Mylan, Marta Montoro and Eileen Moore. Other readers whose feedback was extremely helpful were Neyde Trindade, Michael Shellenberger, Elaine Katzenberger and Norman Solomon. We would especially like to thank our publisher Food First Books, in particular Marilyn Borchardt for her enthusiastic support.

We would never have been able to embark on this project without the generous assistance of several friends, particularly Kit Miller, Susanne Browne, Richard Siemans and Eric Leenson from Progressive Asset Management. Thanks to Bluma Cohen from the Jarulzelsky Foundation for her encouragement.

For research support, we thank Beto Borges, with the Rainforest Action Network; Caius Brandão, with the International Child Resource Institute; and Tarcisio Costa, consul adjunct at the Brazilian Consulate in San Francisco. In Brazil, photographer Jorge Nunes was extremely helpful in letting us dig into his precious archive.

This book has already sparked a series of exchanges between Brazilian and U.S. women. We are grateful to Cecilia dos Santos, Marcia Meireles, Sueli Carneiro, Jurema Werneck and Maria José Araújo for helping us contact the women's groups in Brazil. We have received encouragement and support from many women's organizations, as well as from the John D. and Catherine T. MacArthur Foundation.

Finally, we'd like to thank Benedita da Silva, for so generously sharing with us her life, her thoughts, and her dreams. We hope we have done justice to them.

Introduction

This book is based on a series of interviews with Benedita da Silva, or Bené, as she is affectionately known. Bené is the first poor, black woman from the *favelas,* the shantytowns, to become a major political figure in Brazil. By recounting her amazing odyssey from Rio's *favelas* to the nation's Senate, the book brings to life one of Brazil's most popular political figures.

Going to bed hungry as a child and then watching her own children go hungry, Bené portrays the tragedy of Brazil's poor. Fighting to bring water and electricity to her *favela* and then becoming a founding member of the Workers Party, she embodies the strength of Brazilian activists. Rejecting the passive female role and taking the male-dominated world of politics by storm, she represents Brazil's "new woman."

When we first interviewed Bené, it was a lazy Sunday. In her sandals and house dress, she was strolling through the *favela* where she has lived all her life, visiting the Neighborhood Association and trying to arrange a more convenient living situation for a poor, elderly friend who could hardly walk. But the pace picked up as she rushed home to put on an elegant silk suit and called her driver to take her to the luxurious Governor's Palace, where she gave a speech to commemorate 300 years of black resistance to slavery and received an award for her efforts to eliminate racism. From there she was off to a reception at a cultural center for the launching of a book about the lives of four black women artists, but not forgetting to first swing by to pick up her granddaughter Ana Benedita at her ballet school. Bené ended the day by attending evening mass at her church and chatting with the pastor about ongoing church projects. This was a "relaxing Sunday."

To witness Bené's week-day activities, we followed her on the two-hour plane ride from her home in Rio to the nation's capital,

Brasília, where she commutes virtually every week to carry out her duties as Senator. Her typical day in Brasília starts at 8:00 A.M. and ends at about 11:00 P.M. Her time is filled with meetings with everyone from grassroots organizers to businessmen, Senate hearings on critical economic issues and press interviews. There are days when she has no time to eat, warming up a late-night bowl of vegetable soup before dragging herself to bed.

Despite her harried schedule, Bené makes time for her family and friends when she is back home in Rio. We had the pleasure of tasting the Senator's delicious home cooking at a family gathering at her house in the *favela,* where Bené, her son, daughter and husband argued vehemently about soccer teams while the grandchildren danced to funk music on the patio outside. We went to a Christmas potluck party at her office in Rio, where the staff showed their affection by giving her a sexy nightgown for her "romantic nights with Pitanga," her husband.

We accompanied Bené in moments of joy, like the wedding of one of her advisors, where she delivered a moving speech about love conquering all. There were also moments of great sorrow, like the funeral for a young mother from Bené's *favela* who died from an intestinal obstruction that was misdiagnosed and mistreated at a public hospital for the poor.

We witnessed Bené's strong spiritual side when we watched her at church and community activities organized by her pastor. On the surface, her conservative Evangelical religion seems to clash with her progressive political views. In fact, many of her colleagues in the Workers Party remain baffled by her religious affiliation. Only after hearing her entire life story did we begin to understand this apparent contradiction.

We were struck by the graceful way Bené moves in and out of the most diverse circles imaginable. In a gathering of blacks or whites, men or women, rich or poor, Bené holds her ground with great dignity. In the Senate, she is mostly surrounded by rich, white men. Although she fights them tooth and nail on economic policies, she greets them with a broad smile. She moves with ease from an austere Evangelical church service in a white, middle-class suburb to a meeting of leaders in the black movement.

To try to grasp Bené's complexities, we supplemented the interviews with archival material. We poured through newspaper clippings and transcripts of the political speeches she has made over the years. We interviewed Bené's friends, family, advisors and the public at large. The result is an intriguing mix of her personal experiences with her political vision.

While famous in Brazil, Bené is virtually unknown to U.S. audiences. But then again, so is Brazil. Most Americans know about Rio's Carnival, Pelé and his soccer feats, and perhaps the destruction of the Amazon rain forest. They may have even heard of the plight of Brazil's street children.

Hidden, however, is the vibrant political life of this vast nation. Hidden are the political parties that present a greater range of opinion than our own, the plethora of non-governmental organizations that have created a vigorous "civil society," the women like Benedita da Silva who have challenged Brazil's *macho* culture and shattered gender stereotypes. We hope that this book helps unmask the "real Brazil." By publishing the book simultaneously in English and Portuguese, we also hope to stimulate new ties between people in the U.S. and Brazil who are seeking creative ways to address poverty, racism, gender inequalities and other social problems.

We hope this book does justice to a woman who is one of Brazil's most popular political figures and offers a ray of hope for so many of her nation's poor.

Chapter One
My Life, My Loves

Photo by Jorge Nunes

Benedita with her grandchildren in Copacabana

M y life story is like a samba by Neguinho da Beija Flor that says:

"Se eu pudesse dar um toque	"If I could change my destiny I
em meu destino, não seria	wouldn't be a wanderer in
um peregrino nesse	this harsh world
imenso mundo cão.	
Um bom menino que vendeu	As a good kid who worked in
limão, trabalhou na feira	the market, selling lemons
pra ganhar o pão.	to earn his daily bread
Não aprendia as maldades que	I didn't repeat the cruelties I
essa vida tem.	learned from life
Mataria a minha fome sem ter	I can feed myself without
que roubar ninguém.	robbing anyone
Juro que não pertencia à famosa	I swear I didn't belong in those
funabem onde foi minha	infamous orphanages
morada desde o tempo de	where I lived since I was a
neném.	baby
É ruim acordar de madrugada	It's hard to wake up at dawn to
pra vender bala no trem.	sell candy in the train
Se pudesse tocar em meu	If I could change my destiny I
destino, hoje eu seria	would be somebody,
alguém.	
Seria eu um intelectual,	I would be an intellectual

mas como não tive sorte de ter estudado num colégio legal,	But since I wasn't lucky enough to get a good education
hoje me chamam pivete, mas nunca me deram apoio moral.	Today I'm called a punk and no one gives me moral support
Se eu pudesse não seria um problema social."	If I had an option I wouldn't be a social problem."

Tocar no meu destino—change my destiny—that's exactly what I did. When I think about everything I've been through in my life, I feel so blessed that I was able to change my destiny.

When I look back at my life, I first think of my parents. My mother and father, José and Ovidia, met when they were children and fell in love. But my mother's family didn't let them get married because he was a peasant and had nothing. When my mother was 13, she had to marry a man named Benjamin, who was 40 years old and had his own farm. She invited her girlfriends over her house all the time and all she wanted to do was play—after all, she was just a girl. She didn't know anything about getting pregnant and giving birth, and her first two daughters, Luarita and Sindoca, almost died.

Her marriage didn't last very long because Benjamin got sick and died. His family didn't allow my mother to inherit anything. Perhaps they knew that she and my father always liked each other. They ended up getting married a few years later.

Since my father had no land and my mother was left with nothing, they had to work as day laborers on a *fazenda* in Minas Gerais. They were treated like slaves—they worked in exchange for food and they weren't free to leave. The working conditions on the *fazenda* were horrible, and the food they received wasn't enough to feed all the children. So after many years my mother decided to take all 12 of her children and run away to Rio de Janeiro.

My father, José, stayed in Minas. He told my mother that she was crazy. She didn't have any money, she didn't know anyone in

Rio, she had 12 children and was pregnant. But my mother said, "No, José, I'm not crazy. You'll see. We're going to get a house and when it's all set up, I'll send for you." And that's just what she did.

It was 1936 when my mother moved to Rio and set up a shack in a *favela,* a shantytown, called Praia do Pinto. To make money she opened a *birosca*—a little store front—and washed clothes. As soon as she managed to get a bigger shack, she sent for my father. As you can see, my family is very matriarchal. It's the women who are the risk-takers and the ones who make the decisions—the women in my family are fearless.

I was born in the *favela* Praia do Pinto on March 11, 1943. I was only a few months old when we soon moved to another *favela* called Chapéu Mangueira, where I've remained all my life.

My mother had 13 children in all, but I only knew eight of them. The others died of different diseases like measles and tuberculosis, which used to kill a lot of children in those days. The oldest—Laurita and Sindoca—were from my mother's first marriage; afterwards came Dinha, Roserval, Leda, Tonho, Celeide, and then Ivo. Today, there are only five of us left—Sindoca, Roserval and Tonho died of cancer.

My father worked in construction and he also washed cars. My mother washed clothes, but with the invention of washing machines and dry cleaners, she began to get less and less work.

One of the people my mother washed clothes for was Juscelino Kubitcheck, who later became president of Brazil. Their relationship was like that of master and slave. There was not much dialogue—one gave orders and the other obeyed. I used to go to his house to deliver the laundry and Juscelino's wife would feel sorry for me and give me old clothes and toys that belonged to their daughter Marcia. Actually, the first doll I ever had was Marcia's old doll. I never imagined that I would become a Federal Deputy and meet up with her in Congress—the daughter of the former president and the daughter of the laundry woman!

My mother worked so hard. She was a very strong woman with a lot of energy and I was very proud of her. She was also a very beautiful woman, but unfortunately none of us daughters inherited her looks. She used to laugh and say to my father, "José, watch out. You know how pretty I am." But she drank a lot and ruined her health. José tried to get her to stop drinking but she wouldn't. "You're going to die before me," he'd tell her. Little did he know why she drank so much.

When my mother first moved to Rio and my father was still in Minas, she met the great love of her life. His name was João Modesto Elias, but everyone called him Dadá. He was very sick and my mother took care of him. They eventually fell in love, and I was born as a result of their romance. José had no idea that Dadá was my real father and neither did I. My mother was racked by guilt and began to drink. She also felt threatened by people who knew the truth, like my older sisters. One day, my sisters and mother had a big fight. I didn't know what they were yelling about but then my mother called me in and told me I was Dadá's daughter. She said that if I ever told anyone, she would die.

That night Dadá came over. He told me he was my father and that he liked me very much. I was so confused. I remember that he was eating cheese and put a piece in my mouth. I was disgusted, and burst into tears. But Mother asked me to be nice to him. I was six years old and loved my mother very much. I thought she was the greatest. I didn't want to do anything to hurt her.

One day, on *Dia de Reis* — All Kings Day, a group of musicians and singers were going from door to door telling the story of Jesus's birth. Some came dressed as clowns, carrying flags and dancing. They came into my house, and I saw that Dadá was with them, playing an accordion. When everyone left, my mother got drunk and cried a lot. Dadá had brought his fiancé along. The same thing happened on the day Dadá got married; my mother got really drunk.

Little by little, Dadá and I became closer. When I was almost seven, he came with a little present and I was surprised because my birthday was more than a month away. He told me that my birthday wasn't April 26, like it said on my birth certificate, but was really March 11. When I was born, my family didn't have money to pay for the birth certificate, so they had to wait. This is very common among poor people in Brazil.

Even though we were poor, my mother understood the importance of education. She wanted me to be a teacher and I wanted to be a doctor. I was better off than my older brothers and sisters because they grew up in the *fazenda* and couldn't go to school. I was the only one in my family who learned how to read and write. At least I was able to go to elementary school, but I couldn't afford to continue until I was much older.

I remember that when I was in school I only had one outfit and I wore it every day. But my mother was very tidy and she'd make sure I was always be neat and clean. Even so, the other kids made fun of me.

Shoes were very expensive, and I had to wear second-hand shoes. I had these awful, clunky shoes with metal cleats on the soles that made a horrible noise. Everybody would laugh when they heard the clunk, clunk, clunk, because they'd know it was me. My feet were so big that the shoes were always too tight for me. I'd get these big callouses, and they'd hurt like crazy. Sometimes I'd have to cut off the tips of my shoes so I could walk. Even today, I have problems with my feet from wearing such terrible shoes.

We used to make our own underwear. Sometimes, when we didn't have a needle and thread, we'd just take a piece of cloth and tie a knot on each side, like a diaper. I'll never forget how humiliated I was one day in school when my underpants started to fall. The whole school was out on the patio singing the national anthem, like we did every day before class began. I felt my underwear falling, so I stood with my legs pressed tightly together and didn't move. Then the teacher began to call us back in, class by class. When she called my class, I didn't have a choice. I began to walk and my underpants fell off in front of everyone. It was the most embarrassing moment of my life. From then on, when the kids saw me coming, they'd say, *"Sua calça caiu, sua mãe não viu!"* — Your underwear's hanging down, your mother's not around.

By the time I was seven, I was already out working. I shined shoes, and I sold candy, peanuts, and fruit in the marketplace. I learned early on the prejudices against girls. The market venders didn't want to hire us because they said we weren't as strong as boys and it would take us twice as long to carry the boxes to and from the market. I insisted on proving that I could work as hard as the boys did. That's when they started calling me macho woman — a reputation I have to this day.

I was a street kid, out hustling all day long, but at night I'd go home to sleep. It was important for me to keep my family ties. Even if you live in a cardboard shack, your home is your home. The most important thing is to have someplace to go back to.

Some of my relatives didn't like the fact that I was out on the streets all day. When I was 10, they discovered that I smoked and it was quite a scandal. When I'd go visit my cousins, my aunts and uncles would say, *"a filha da Ovidia é uma perdida"* — Ovidia's daughter is a lost cause. But my cousins, Ana and Ceição, would always give me the warmest welcome. They'd say, "Dita's here!" They would love to hear me tell stories about the things I saw and heard on the streets. There was not much dialogue between parents and children in those days. So we'd talk among ourselves about sex and other secrets.

I loved sleeping at my cousin's house. We'd curl up in the bed together to talk. The only problem was that they always peed in the bed, and the sheets would get all wet and cold. I'd get up early, before their parents were awake, and fix up the bed because if their parents found out, my poor cousins would get a spanking.

My mother was a midwife and one of the most exciting things for me was to go with her when she was delivering a baby. She'd make me stay outside, but I would peek in and see everything. The most amazing part was when she'd remove the placenta. After a baby was born, people would always say that the stork brought it. But I didn't believe them; I never saw a single stork.

I had a hard time believing in Santa Claus, too. The night before Christmas I would leave my stocking on the window sill before going to bed, but the next day, it would be empty. How I cried! My parents would say that Santa didn't come because I'd been naughty, and that if I improved my behavior, he would come the next year. They preferred to keep the myth alive than to say that Santa Claus didn't exist and that we didn't have presents because we were too poor.

This was my routine when I was a child: At five o'clock in the morning I'd get up and go to the well to gather water. At 6:30 I'd go to work at the market, and go to school at noon. After school, I 'd go from house to house collecting bundles of clothes for my mother to wash, or gathering charcoal and wood. In the evening, I'd go home to study.

I never had much time to play, but we street children had our own games. I loved to make carts. We'd take the boxes the fish came in, because they were very strong, cut a slat in each side, and attach wheels to them. Then we'd have races down the hills. I'd also use the carts to do errands—carrying bags in the market, bringing the laundry to my mother, fetching water.

To carry the water buckets, we also made balances out of broom handles, with hooks on both ends. We carried them across our shoulders, two buckets at a time, but they had to weigh the same. My mother taught me how to place the buckets just right so that I wouldn't hurt my back or get my clothes wet or spill water. The more I grew, the larger the buckets I carried. When I was six years old, I carried five liters; when I was eight, I carried 10 liters; and when I was 10, I reached the maximum weight, which was 20 liters.

Spending so much time on the street, I suffered from all kinds of harassment. The men would grab us girls, they'd put their hands on our behinds and touch our breasts. The men would try to get us to become prostitutes, and many girls would give in. This happened to my sister Dinha. She was very pretty, but she was a tough cookie. People called her Dinha Madeira, or Wooden Dinha, because if a man gave her a hard time, she'd hit him and knock him down. My mother accepted the fact that she was a prostitute, but my father was furious and kicked her out of the house.

I always resisted becoming a prostitute, but I had a deep secret that traumatized me from a very early age. I've never told anyone about this, not even my close family. It was horrible. There was this guy, Adão, who was a friend of the family and lived in our house for years. He raped both me and my cousin. I was seven when it started and my cousin was 14.

Our house only had two bedrooms. My parents slept in one room, and all the kids slept in the other. When Adão was living with us, he slept in the room with the kids. He would wait until everyone was asleep and then he'd come to my bed. My brothers and sisters never knew what was happening. I wanted to scream, but I was afraid. I was so young. He had this horrible smell, and it made me want to vomit. He smelled like bedbugs, because his shirt was full of bugs.

I suffered a lot but no one knew, not even my cousin. We never talked about it. She got pregnant and had a very traumatic abortion. She bled all day long and almost died. I watched the whole thing and was terrified.

I really wanted my mother to find out what this guy was doing to me, but I couldn't bring myself to tell her. So I pretended I had a infection in my vagina and asked her to take me to the doctor. She took me, but the doctor didn't say anything. I never had a chance to tell her that Adão was getting into my bed to do nasty things to me. He finally moved out but he left me very traumatized.

My mother never talked to me about sex, even though she was a midwife. When I first got my period, she called in a *"mulher da vida,"* as we called prostitutes in those days, to come talk to me. Her name was Aparecida and she always hung out at my house. Aparecida told me, "Don't let any boys play around with you anymore, because now you're a woman and you can get pregnant." She told me everything my mother was too embarrassed to say. But I already knew everything. I knew what menstruation was, I knew about sex because I used to peek though the keyhole to spy on my sister with her boyfriend. I learned everything by watching, listening and reading. My experience growing up on the streets was difficult but it was also a school—a school of life where you learn everything.

My youth was also difficult because I was such an ugly duckling. I was so big and it didn't help that my mother would put my hair in these horrible braids. There was a lot of racism and the kids would pull my hair and call me *nega maluca,* a crazy nigger. And they said I looked like a giraffe because I was so tall. The boys didn't want to go out with me. My only consolation was that I was a great dancer and when I went to dances, the boys always wanted to dance with me. But that's the only time they paid attention to me.

The first boy who looked at me was my cousin, Mané Matola. Mané had a crush on me and he'd come to our house with little presents. I loved to dance with him but I didn't really like him as a boyfriend. Besides, my family didn't allow cousins to marry. So I'd say: "Mané, I'm not the one for you. Go find someone else."

I fell in love for the first time when I was 14 years old. He was a very charming, older boy who lived nearby and always came to visit us. His name was Sebastião Nunes da Silva but we called him Cuty. He was a distant cousin of mine. We used to dance together in the samba school. I was crazy about him, but he thought I was just a little girl, not old enough to be a girlfriend. He knew I adored him and would take advantage of it, but I never slept with him. In those days you didn't have sex before marriage.

One day Cuty brought a girlfriend to my house. I was devastated. He said, "Don't be sad. You're just a kid, don't you understand?" He really hurt my feelings, but he was also the one who first made me feel like a woman. Two years later when I got married, Cuty came to my wedding. We danced a waltz together because my husband didn't know how to dance, and he whispered in my ear, "You are so beautiful. I know you don't really love him. You're just marrying him to get back at me." And I said, "I do love him. And I feel sorry for you because you had hit the jackpot and you didn't even know it."

But the truth is, I was still madly in love with him. Every day I'd go by his house and hide at the corner to see if I could get a glimpse of him. It took me a long time to get him out of my mind. It was only when his girlfriend Elsa got pregnant that I knew I had to forget about him. Once I finally got him out of my system, I realized that he would be the last man on earth that I would want to marry.

As an adolescent, I felt the need to get closer to my biological father, Dadá. He washed cars in Copacabana, and I would visit him at work without anyone knowing. I needed his emotional support, because my mother's health was deteriorating.

My mother had a strong sense of intuition and when she realized she was going to die, she called me and said, "Never ask Dadá for anything." And I never did. When I married, he wanted to give me presents and I said, "I don't need any because my father José already gave me some."

In 1957 my mother died. I was devastated. I was only 15, and I missed her terribly. I wrote a poem for her that goes like this:

Minha mãe	My mother
que pariu treze filhos	who gave birth to 13 children
que fugiu da roça	who escaped from the countryside
pra morar no Rio	to live in Rio
pra ser lavadeira	to do laundry
freqüentar gafieira	to dance *gafieira*
pra bater tambor	to play drums
pra abrir birosca	to sell food
pra tomar cachaça	to drink *cachaça*
pra rir da desgraça	to laugh at bad times
pra acabar parteira	to be a midwife
no Chapéu Mangueira.	in Chapéu Mangueira.
Minha mãe	My mother
cintura fina	slender waist
parecia um violão	like a guitar
pele linda, de menina	beautiful skin, like a girl
machucando corações	breaking hearts
bem amada, não duvide	well loved, no doubt
há provas	we have proof
estou aqui.	here I am.

The years after my mother's death were very difficult. I continued to live with my father José and my younger brother Ivo. Our financial situation got worse, because my mother had contributed a lot to the family pot. Ivo managed to get a job in a bookstore and Dinha, who had worked as a prostitute, changed her life, came back home and got a job in a laundromat. I started working as a volunteer on community literacy and health projects with some of the people in the Catholic Church, and would get some help from them.

Just when our financial situation started to get better, Ivo lost his job. He continued to do odd jobs here and there, but it was never enough and he started stealing. When my father found out, he kicked him out of the house. I couldn't believe it! As a child, Ivo was the family's pride and joy, and we all took care of him. Then he became a pickpocket and everyone became ashamed of him. I felt sorry for him and continued to bring him food every now and then, but I never told my father.

One day, after my mother had died, I got in a terrible argument with my sister Celeide and she told my father about Dadá. He was very angry and said he would kill him. Everyone was shouting at each other, and my father said I should go live with Dadá. My older brother, Roserval, didn't let me go and said he would care for me. My father eventually relented, because he loved me and deep down inside, he didn't want me to go. Perhaps it was more a question of hurt pride. I continued to live with him even after I was married, but I never stopped visiting Dadá.

I was 16 when I met the man who became my first husband. His name was Nilton Aldano da Silva, but everyone called him Mansinho, because he walked slowly. He worked hard as a handyman and a house painter.

We started to go out together and we got married eight months later, on December 26, 1958. He was 10 years older than me and he'd grown up on the streets, too. But unlike me, he'd lost contact with his family and only found them again after we got married. He grew up in a government orphanage, which is a place where a lot of children learn how to be criminals. But Mansinho was different, he was hard-working.

I continued my activities in the community, working with the neighborhood association, organizing literacy classes and trying to improve the health conditions. Mansinho didn't get involved himself, but he didn't try to stop me. In fact, he'd help out in the house when I had to go to meetings.

Mansinho also helped me grow as a woman. I was still traumatized from being raped and I needed to have a good partner to feel pleasure from sex. After we had sex together for the first time, I told him that I'd been raped. He said he didn't want to know who did it, and we never talked about it again.

It was in that relationship that I learned that sex was a marvelous thing. I had a different experience than the most young girls because Mansinho taught me to enjoy sex. He even taught me to take initiative in sexual relations, which was something totally unusual in those days.

We didn't use contraceptives back then. I got pregnant for the first time when I was 17 . . . but I lost my son. His name was Carlos Eduardo, and he died after eight days from something called *"mau de umbigo,"* which is an infection of the umbilical cord. He was born at home and by the time I got him to the hospital, it was too late. If I hadn't been so poor, he wouldn't have died. I would have taken him to the hospital right away and they could have cured him. I suffered terribly looking at the little clothes that I'd collected with so much sacrifice. He was such a beautiful child.

Three months later I was pregnant again and this time my daughter Nilcea was born. At first I didn't know I was pregnant because I continued to menstruate. I lost a lot of blood during that pregnancy. I think it was from doing things like carrying buckets of water on my head. But what could I do? I had to keep working.

When I was in labor, I went to the hospital to give birth this time. I was in horrible pain and they made me wait forever. I could tell that the baby was ready to come out and I desperately called for the nurse. She said that someone was in the delivery room and I'd have to wait. She also didn't believe I was ready to give birth and tried to close my legs. I kept myself from screaming but I grabbed her arm with such force that I hurt her. I ended up having the baby before I even got to the delivery room. Afterwards, she yelled at me for hurting her and I told her, "What did you want me to do? My baby was coming out and you were trying to close my legs!"

A year later I got pregnant again and after seven months I began to lose blood. One day the hemorrhaging got really bad and I had to go to the hospital. I remember that I had no clean clothes to put on, because I didn't have any soap to wash with. I grabbed a wet skirt from the wash basin and ran outside. My neighbor Rita went to call an ambulance. The ambulance never came and I didn't have money to pay the bus fare. The baby was born premature, and died two days later. We didn't even have money to give him a proper burial. I thought I would go crazy; it was more than I could bear.

When I was 20, my son Leleco was born. He was not a healthy baby and he got meningitis when he was eight months old. That was another agonizing time because he was in a coma for two weeks. Luckily he survived, but he had trouble learning in school as a result of his illness.

I always had difficult pregnancies and I'm sure it's related to the fact that we were so hungry and poor. There were times when we ate from the trash cans at restaurants. So when I became pregnant for the fifth time, I didn't know how I could possibly feed another child and decided to have an abortion.

The abortion was a painful experience and I profoundly regret having done it. The decision was my own, my husband didn't say anything, either pro or con, and in those days I didn't have a spiritual conviction to stop me. I felt really pressured by people who said that I shouldn't have more children because I was too poor. So I went to a woman who does clandestine abortions. I regretted it as soon as I began hemorrhaging, but it was already too late. That botched abortion ruined my health and caused me much physical and emotional pain. I lost my uterus and had to be operated on seven times, and I've suffered from severe hormonal imbalances ever since.

My two surviving children, Nilcea and Leleco, were raised practically without a mother. I was so busy trying to feed them that I didn't have time to spend with them. My husband and I were out working all the time. My children grew up knowing that they had to take care of themselves, they had to find their own path. And since I had to choose between being home to take care of them or going out hustling to get food for them, I always felt very guilty.

I'd go to get porridge for the children from the church of Sister Teresa, and we'd all share it because it was often the only food we had. Sometimes I'd eat manioc flour with sugar and then drink water to fill up my stomach. Other times I would fry sardines with oxen oil. I had to close up the entire house so the neighbors wouldn't smell the horrible odor. I also cooked potato skin, pumpkin buds, I made stewed papaya. . . . And when we were hungry and had absolutely nothing, we'd wrap a tight cloth around our bellies to take away the pain.

Food got more expensive when it became packaged, and supermarkets began to appear. Before, we were always able to find something in the market. We'd collect the rice left at the bottom of the sack, or beans or pasta that had fallen on the ground.

It was agonizing to look at the empty pots and then have to face my children. My husband Mansinho never had a steady job, especially when it rained and he couldn't work as a house painter. He used to say with pride that he never robbed anyone during all his years as a street kid, but if one day there was no food for our children, he would go out and steal it. So I had to make sure that he never knew when there was no food in the house. And the children went along with me. If my husband asked them if they had eaten, they'd say yes. Then they'd go off to bed hungry.

Sometimes we'd get help from a wonderful friend, Marcela, who was Leleco's godmother. She was about 10 years older than me, and she knew me from the time I was born. We'd always see each other at the samba school Unidos do Leme. But we really became close friends after my mother died. She became like a mother to me. She was the only person I told that we didn't have food at home; I was too ashamed to even tell my sisters. When things were really bad, I'd go to her house and tell her that I didn't have any food to give the children. Sometimes she would stop eating and give me her plate of food to bring to the kids. She knew that I loved fish soup, and when she could afford it, she'd make us soup and bring it over the house. She'd also go with me to church when they were giving out free food.

Marcela died two years ago, and I feel terrible that I wasn't able to do more for her. I would have liked to have paid for her funeral, but I found out too late. I wasn't even able to go to the funeral because I was out of town. To this day, I still regret it.

Nilcea and Leleco began to work at an early age. Nilcea cleaned houses and Leleco delivered bread early in the morning. Leleco later got a job at the Leme Tennis Club picking up the tennis balls. He was 11 when he got his first work permit. He was always very responsible, using his money to buy food and other things for the family.

Although we were dirt poor, I always loved to have a clean house, a nicely made bed. There were times when we had no furniture, and I'd put a piece of wood on four tin cans, lay some newspaper on top, and that's where we'd sleep. But it was all nice and neat. I'd make pretty designs out of newspaper to decorate the walls. I'd clean the pots with ashes until they shined like mirrors. I never allowed poverty to be equated with dirtiness. My children only had one set of clothes for going out and one for sleeping. So every night I'd wash the clothes for them to wear the next day.

I also had a strong sense of morality. For example, no matter how bad things got, I would never sell my body. Many women did, but I would do anything else but that. I'd shine shoes, clean floors, sell clothes, work in the market, anything.

I was good at doing domestic work, but during that time it was very difficult work because maids had no rights. The women of the house dealt directly with the maids, and this was one of the things that gave these rich or middle-class women some power. They wanted show their husbands that their maids worked hard for little money. The needs of the workers were rarely taken into consideration.

When I was single I'd work as a live-in maid and only come home once every two weeks. It was terrible work because there were no set hours. When you worked as a live-in maid, you had to work all day and night. My bosses would always tell me that I was part of the family. What a joke! I don't know what family member would agree to be treated like a slave.

After I got married and had children, I stopped working as a live-in maid and only cleaned house during the day. I'd never take my children to work with me. I knew that when women took their children to work, the children ended up doing free labor for the family and I didn't want that to happen. So I'd leave my kids home by themselves, even when they were little. I was always worried to death, thinking that something terrible was happening to them. I'd listen to the radio all the time, in case there was news about some children getting hurt.

It was very humiliating work. Sometimes my boss would say that she forgot to go to the bank and couldn't pay me. I'd leave the house with a piece of hard bread to give my children and I'd have to go home and make bread soup.

I remember one time when a woman I worked for came into the kitchen and found me talking to my sister. My sister had come to ask for help because her husband had just died. The woman didn't bother to ask what had happened and instead started yelling, "I don't like this. Your sister shouldn't be here." That same day I gave her house a thorough cleaning, went home and never came back.

I still think about those days when I worked as a maid. Just a while ago I was eating dinner at the home of a woman ambassador and I heard her comment to one of the guests: "Look how elegantly she eats!" And I thought, "Of course. I learned from serving your food!" I spent a lot of time serving the rich. I was the one who set the table, who cooked the food, who cleaned up. The only thing I didn't do was sit at the table and eat the food.

For a long time, I worked as a domestic servant, but then I got really tired of it and looked for other work. I worked as a street vendor, selling food, clothes, cosmetics, everything you can imagine. I worked at a leather belt factory and as a janitor at a school. In 1975, when I was in my early thirties, I landed a government job in the Department of Transportation, working as a clerk. And in 1979, I took a nurse's aide course and supplemented my income by getting a part-time job in the Miguel Couto Hospital.

I always felt insecure because I never had a chance to finish high school. So I decided that I would study at home and then take the high school equivalency exam. I borrowed textbooks from Danilo, one of the neighborhood kids, and studied in the early hours of the morning. I could teach myself everything but math. Luckily, I managed to get Danilo to come over and help me.

This was my routine: I'd leave early in the morning to work at the Department of Transportation, then I'd go to my job at the hospital. I'd come home completely exhausted, but I'd force myself to study. The only reason I was able to do all this was that Nilcea helped me tremendously by taking charge of the house.

Sometimes I just couldn't get to class and I'd miss an exam. Other times, I would go to class without even knowing that we were having a test. One day, I got to class and a friend warned me, "Bené, we have an exam today." I was totally unprepared and I said, "Oh, my God, what am I going to do?" She said, "Here, take this," and she handed me a cheat sheet. And wouldn't you know it. The one time in my life that I cheated, I got caught. In front of everyone, the teacher took away my exam and yelled at me. I was mortified. Can you imagine? A 40-year-old getting caught cheating.

With a lot of sacrifice, I managed to get my high school diploma in 1980, and I enrolled in the university to study social work. In fact, my daughter Nilcea and I went to college at the same time — I was 40 and she was 20. My children and husband Mansinho were great — they always encouraged me to continue my studies.

In that sense, my husband was very good to me. He adored me

and supported my efforts to study and get a better job. And during all the years we were together, he always supported my community work. Other women's husbands would give them a hard time when they wanted to go out to neighborhood meetings at night, but not Mansinho. Whether it was organizing in the community or studying to get ahead, Mansinho encouraged me.

But life was not easy for him; he had a serious problem with alcohol. Mansinho would always promise us that he'd stop drinking, and then a half hour later he'd come home drunk. He really had a sickness. Nilcea and I started going to Alcoholics Anonymous meetings because when he'd drink, he'd start fighting with us. Nilcea was like me, she was tough and independent. My son Leleco was quieter; he didn't fight with his father.

Just when I was getting better jobs and our lives were starting to improve, Mansinho had a stroke. He was only 45 years old. From one day to the next my world started to fall apart.

I clearly remember that day. We were at home and Mansinho was cooking rice and chicken for dinner, and having his usual drink of *cachaça*. Suddenly, he felt very sick and almost fainted. We took him to the hospital where I worked. It was Sunday and I stayed with him all day. The next day, when he was feeling better, I went home and Nilcea came to stay with him. A few hours later Nilcea called me and told me that Mansinho was having trouble speaking. I said, "What? When I left him a few hours ago he was up and about. He was in the bathroom shaving!" I went running to the hospital. When I got there he had just had another stroke.

I'll never forget what he told me when I got to the hospital. He said, *"Você é fora de série"* — You're one of a kind. It was always hard for him to express his feelings, because growing up on the streets was such a bitter experience for him. But I understood what he wanted to say and I answered, *"Você é que é muito legal"* — You're the one who's really great.

He thought he didn't deserve my attention during the time he was sick because I'd always told him to stop drinking and take care of his health. But I stayed with him the whole time. I was desperate. He got worse and worse and the next morning he was in a coma. I was working in the same hospital and I was on duty, so my sisters took me home to get my uniform. I hurried back to the hospital but by the time I got there, he had just died. It was awful. We'd spent 22 years together—a whole lifetime. I couldn't imagine life without him.

After Mansinho died, I started to get more involved in community work with the Neighborhood Association in Chapéu Mangueira. The president of the Association, Agnaldo Bezerra dos Santos, was a great community leader. He was one of the founders of the Neighborhood Federation of the State of Rio and everyone knew him as Bola. He was a both a Christian and a communist. He was affiliated with the Communist Party and also worked with the Christian-based communities in the *favelas.*

Bola had made his living as a boxer and then as a chauffeur. But now he had health problems and was retired. We'd been friends for many years. After I was widowed, I tried to avoid spending much time with him. I was friends with his wife Baleca and I didn't want people to start talking. But everything happened very fast. Baleca died a few months after Mansinho did. It was a very difficult time for both of us and we tried to give each other support. We talked about how much we missed our companions and we cried a lot together.

One evening at a Neighborhood Association meeting, he passed me a note saying: "Are you flirting with me?" We joked about it, but nothing happened until six months later when he asked me to go out with him. It wasn't long before he started talking about marriage, but I thought it was still early. Bola had five children and although they were already grown up, he was very dedicated to them. We both had many responsibilities with our children, and they were jealous of us spending so much time together.

In the meantime, I started branching out from my work in the

Neighborhood Association to working with a new political party that was being formed, called the Workers Party. It was 1982 and this new party decided to run candidates in the upcoming elections. My friends in the Neighborhood Association encouraged me to run for City Council, and Bola offered to coordinate my campaign. To our amazement, we won the election and I became the first Workers Party representative in Rio.

After the campaign Bola became my chief political advisor and we worked together on our political strategies. He always respected my ideas and my wishes; he was the kind of man who never argued with women.

Six months later, we decided to get married. I was 41 and he was 45. We made our decision one day when we were returning from a meeting and stopped to take a walk along the beach. It wasn't an easy decision, because we both had a lot of obligations to our children, the church, and the community. But we decided to make the commitment and share our lives; it was a beautiful moment for both of us.

We got married on January 26, 1983. Pastor Mozart Noronha conducted the ceremony in the Lutheran Church of Ipanema. It was the first time Bola was married in a church, and he was very nervous. We had a very beautiful wedding, and the whole community participated.

After the wedding, Bola came to live with me and my children. His three younger children—Nido, Vandinha, and Arnaldo— were still single and came to live with us. His married daughter Nicinha stayed at his house.

Soon after, we were hit with a horrible tragedy. We found out that Bola's son Arnaldo had cancer. He was 22 years old and was a physical education teacher. He was so beautiful and so strong, but suddenly he began to feel pain in his shoulder. When we took him to the doctor, we discovered that he had lung cancer. It was unbelievable. His health began to deteriorate so fast and six months later, he died. We were all devastated.

My relationship with Bola was filled with much love and mutual support. I was totally crazy about him. He was a great companion—like a big teddy bear—and we were like two love birds. Our friends said we were like the couple on *Casal 20,* the TV show where the husband and wife always do everything together. But fate didn't allow us to enjoy our happiness for long. I had a bad feeling that something was going to happen, because a fortune teller once told me that God was going to take my husband away and something told me she was right. He had high blood pressure and he had already had two heart attacks.

It was Christmas Eve, 1988. We were in the middle of remodeling our house, so Bola went to spend the holiday with his daughter Nicinha, who he adored, and I went to my daughter Nilcea's house. We were going to meet up later in the evening. While I was at my daughter's house I had an accident—I fell down the stairs. So I went home early. I called Bola before I went to sleep. I was worried about him because he was on a special diet and medical treatment, and I wanted to make sure that he had taken his medication. But he assured me that he was fine. I remember that I was listening to Milton Nascimento singing the Christmas mass on TV and I was about to go to sleep when Bola's daughter called and said he was feeling sick. I ran over to her house and we rushed him to the hospital. But it was too late.

I couldn't believe that Bola was dead. We'd only been married five years, but they were very intense years. I was devastated by his sudden death, as were his family and friends. He was very loved by everyone in the community, and over 600 people came to his funeral.

The first day I returned to my office after Bola's death was horrible. Many people thought I wouldn't continue my political work without him. Bola had such a strong personality that everyone thought *he* was the political figure, not me. They saw me as the wife of Bola and thought I would leave politics. But among the things Bola taught me was how to be strong under pressure, and I decided to keep on going. I really missed him, but I felt his energy within me and I forged ahead. How proud he would have been to see me go on to become a Federal Deputy and then a Senator!

I miss both of my husbands, each one was special. Sometimes I see them in my dreams and I want to talk to them.

After Bola died I didn't want to be with any man, and I decided to bury myself in my political work. I also became closer to Dadá. He couldn't work anymore because he suffered from bleeding ulcers, so I began to help him financially. I bought him a house in Caxias, and he moved there with his wife, Maria. Three years later Maria died, and now he has a new companion, whose name is also Maria. Maria was also my mother's real name, even though she went by the name Ovidia.

During the time I was widowed, I met a guy from Africa and we started to date. But it didn't take long for me to realize that it wasn't going to work because he was so sexist! It was a real culture shock. He was a traditional Muslim and thought I acted like a man. He believed that when men spoke, women should be quiet, and that women shouldn't express their opinions in public. I told him, "No way, my dear, that's not my style!" We broke up after a few months. It's too bad because African men are so beautiful, so interesting. Some are short, some are skinny, but they're all charming and they dance with that special swing. But imagine marrying a Muslim who has a bunch of wives? I would never tolerate that.

I stayed single for several years and it was a difficult time for me. It's very sad to be widowed. I began to feel the need to have a partner but no one approached me. I would ask myself, "Is it that I'm so ugly? I don't understand. I take care of myself, I look nice and clean, I'm financially independent. So why can't I meet a good man?" I wanted a partner, someone to warm up my bed. It wasn't a question of sex; I felt the need for companionship.

I talked about this a lot with my two good friends—Neilda,

who's one of my political advisors, and Dai, my hairdresser. We were all the in the same boat. We were three marvelous, independent women, but men were afraid to get close to us. I would joke with them that I was going to put a classified ad in the paper. People actually do that these days, but back then it was unheard of.

We'd go out with guys, but being good feminists, we always made sure we paid our share of the check. The men would complain, "I don't understand this feminism thing. Can't we even be gentleman? Can't we open the door for you? Can't we pay the check?"

I also talked a lot to another friend, my advisor Cicera, who knows me well. Cicera gave me a book called "Women Who Attract Men and Women Who Don't." This book helped me understand what my problem was. I realized that I was imposing feminist demands on my personal relationships. I was the "all powerful" one, I didn't show the slightest bit of dependence or need. The problem is that men don't feel useful when women don't need them. They have the impression they're being slighted.

My social position as a political figure also interfered with my relations during that time. Men don't like women who have important jobs and earn more money than they do.

I was also always looking for the ideal man, and that meant I really didn't notice the good qualities in the men around me. I realized that I'd been making too many demands on men. For example, when I was living with Bola and he spent a lot of time with his children, I'd be unhappy that he was dividing his attention. And I was difficult to live with because I was obsessed with neatness, everything had to be in its place.

So I read that book and I thought, "Oh, dear. Does this mean I'm going to have to put up with a man who throws his dirty underwear on the floor and doesn't do the dishes?" But seriously, that book influenced me and made me realize how demanding I'd been.

I decided to change my tactics. I learned to give in on certain issues and not to be so overbearing. This doesn't mean that I've become submissive, but I've learned to be more flexible and understanding.

But even then it wasn't easy to find anyone interesting. There were not many men my age who were single, and I don't like to go out with younger men. I've always been involved with older men. My friends think I have a hang up about this, but the problem is that most relationships with younger men don't last. In the beginning everything seems fine, but later on the man starts to demand that you act like an adolescent. The problem is not really a sexual one, because I believe that experience is useful in some things. After all, *galinha velha é a que dá bom caldo* —the old hen makes the best soup. But younger men want you to have a perfect little body. And then women become ridiculous or hypocrites. Older men are different because physical appearance is not so important after a certain age.

I was beginning to think I'd never get remarried. And then Pitanga came along, with his Bahiano charm, speaking gently . . . with so much warmth and love. I'd met Pitanga during my campaign for Federal Deputy. He was a black actor and supported my candidacy, but he never looked at me like a woman, just a politician. I only saw him as an actor, not a man.

Pitanga soon realized that there was a woman behind the political figure. It was my daughter Nilcea who first noticed that Pitanga was interested in me. She said, "Are you blind? Don't you see anything? Why don't you give it a try?" But I was afraid. He started flirting with me and would say things like, "Oh, you're so beautiful," and I'd answer, "I have a great dressmaker." I thought, "This guy is a man of the world, he runs in fast circles and has all the women he wants. And I'm very old-fashioned, very traditional. I'm not interested in affairs but in marriage." I never thought Pitanga would want to marry me.

But I decided to give it a try and we began to go out. He was three years older than me, and was divorced with two wonderful children, Camila, who was 19, and Rocco, who was 16.

Right at the time we started dating, I took a trip to Philadelphia to represent Brazil at a conference. While I was there I met this really nice American photographer. It was funny because when I was leaving Brazil, I went to say good-bye to Pitanga and he said, "Don't go falling in love with anyone there because I'm going to marry you." But I thought he was just joking around. This photographer and I became good friends and he said that I was a marvelous woman who was hiding herself, that I was afraid of getting involved with a man.

That trip was in 1991, during the time of the Gulf War. When I returned to Brazil, Pitanga said, "Bené, I want to be your Saddam Hussein against all the allies." And that's just what happened. We fell in love and decided to get married.

It's a good thing I married someone from Bahia, because he doesn't feel the need to be that hard kind of man, the macho type. People from Bahia walk with a certain sashay and I love that. I always wanted to have a boyfriend from Bahia, they're famous for their swing.

Pitanga's got style, and he's so good-looking. My friends say that I only like good-looking men. And it's true—all my partners have been handsome.

Our wedding was a beautiful church ceremony and a great big party. I don't care about the social contract, but I do care about the spiritual blessing that sanctifies our union. And the party symbolizes the pleasure you feel sharing that moment with your friends. That's how it was with Pitanga. Our wedding had over 2,000 guests, with a live band and a chorus.

The press went wild criticizing me. They didn't like the idea of a *favelada* having a big wedding in the plush Jockey Club. The reporters would ask me, "Are people from the *favela* coming?" And I'd say, "I don't make that distinction. They're all guests, whether they're from the *favela* or not." The elite panicked because only

Benedita da Silva could take people from the *favela* to such an exclusive place.

Some people ask why I didn't just have the party in the *favela*. But the point is that we have to open these elite spaces to everyone. My friends in the *favela* shouldn't only enter a nice restaurant or a club when it's time to clean up. They're the ones who are responsible for my happiness. They have the right to enjoy my party in a place like the Jockey Club, don't they?

The newspapers also printed ridiculous articles saying that I had made a huge list of the presents I wanted, including things like five televisions. Actually, I didn't get any televisions, but I did get other presents, like a stove and a microwave oven. I deserve them. After all, I spent my whole life cleaning these things for other people. So why shouldn't I get nice presents like other people do?

While many people criticized the wedding party, the truth is that I didn't spend a penny on it. My friends chipped in to give me the reception as a present. A friend who is a businessman, Eduardo Martins, rented the club, my daughter-in-law Michele made the pastries and a friend from church made the wedding cake. It was such a beautiful party and it was my way of sharing my happiness with all my family and friends.

My relationship with Pitanga is very beautiful and complete because we support each other emotionally and politically. In addition to being an actor, he's a member of Rio's City Council. One of the great things he does is to promote cultural events in poor neighborhoods as a way of fostering community participation and pride. Both of us have very busy lives, so our relationship is an equal one. But at the same time we try to find time to be together and enjoy our family. I'm so lucky to have found such a wonderful partner and to be so in love.

I know that many marriages break down because the men and women aren't faithful to each other. I've never been unfaithful and I don't know if my husbands have ever been. When Pitanga gets home late at night, I never worry that he was out with another woman. I think of anything but that, because I'm not obsessed with this fidelity issue and we trust each other. But if he was with another woman I don't want to know about it, because then I would think, *"O que é que ela tem que eu não tenho?"* — What does she have that I don't have? I think I'm the greatest, so why would he look for another woman?

I see myself as a woman who likes to enjoy life in all its stages. There exists this myth that women shouldn't reveal their age, but I don't have any reason to hide my age. I'm 54 now. When I entered menopause, I decided to go on hormone therapy because I wanted to go through this next phase of my life feeling healthy.

I accept this stage of my life with serenity. I try not to gain weight because this is an age where high blood pressure can be a problem and also because I don't want to gain weight, and then go on a diet and look all shriveled up. Sometimes I get hot flashes, but they go away quickly. Sometimes I get moody and irritated, not just because of menopause but also because of the pressure of my work. But Pitanga and the people I work with help cheer me up.

When I'm feeling down I often get dressed up pretty and go out. I never liked to look disheveled, even when I only had one dress and wore it all the time. The other day I was joking with my daughter because we were trying to decide what to wear. I said, "Who'd ever think that one day we would be standing in front of a closet full of clothes trying to decide what to wear?" I never thought I'd have to decide what to cook for dinner because we had so many different kinds of food in the house.

Despite all the suffering I've been through, I consider myself a very privileged woman. It's not because of the material things I've gained, but because I am loved and surrounded by such beautiful people. God always sent me an angel in my most difficult moments. And when you're surrounded by love, it's a lot easier to confront the harsh realities of life.

Chapter Two
A Walk Through the *Favela*

*"Let me take you on a little tour of Chapeu Mangueira,
the favela where I have been living all my life."*

Favela dos rebolados,
sapateados, bem dançados
da lata d'água na cabeça, de mão na
      cintura
de requebrados.

Favela dos patins improvisados
do chinelo que arrasta
do brinquedo quebrado
de gente que sobe e desce
sem medo do escuro,
sem cerca, sem muro
sem vacilação.

Favela que inspira os poetas
que fala pra ela, dela,
da paixão, da despedida,
da volta,
até do fora que levou no salão.
Favela da mulher traída
do malandro que saiu da prisão,
que chega e não acha nada
nem ninguém no
      barracão

Favela salto alto
saia justa e argolão,
sapato bico fino, chapéu de palha
do palito, almofadinha,
da pipa, da cigarra, do balão
Favela dos tambores,
dos terreiros, procissões
dos crentes batendo às portas,
Folia de Reis chegando
pra todo mundo acordar

Favela do papo de caminho
das amarelinhas,
empadas, pastéis e pés de galinha,
caldo de mocotó e aquela feijoadinha.

Favela de ontem e de agora,
tempo que não volta mais
da minha fantasia

Favela of the dancers
who shake their hips and their feet
with buckets of water on their
      head, hands on their waist
shimmying.

Favela of the improvised roller skates
sandals that shuffle
broken toys
people who go up and down
with no fear of the dark,
no fence, no wall
no hesitation.

Favela that inspires the poets
who speak to her, about her
speak of passion, of loss
of returning
and even of the broken heart on the
      dance floor.
Favela of the betrayed woman
of the *malandro* who left prison
and comes back and finds nothing
and nobody home.

Favela of high heels
tight skirt and hoop earrings
pointed shoes, straw hat
toothpick, decked out,
kite, cricket, balloon
Favela of the drums
ceremonies, processions
preachers knocking on doors
carolers arriving
waking everyone up.

Favela chatting along the way
hopscotch
pastries, snacks and chicken feet
calf's soup and that special *feijoada*.

Favela of today and yesterday
time that will never come back
from my fantasy

de fazê-la sorrir,	to make her smile
cantar, brincar,	sing, play
esquecer	forget
e viver.	and live.
Favela, meu tesouro,	*Favela,* my treasure
seu encanto me seduz	your charm seduces me
mesmo sem água e energia tu és feita de	with no water or electricity, you are
luz	still made of light
és minha musa inspiradora, meu lugar,	you're my inspirational muse, my
meu chão	place, my land.
Aguenta firme, Favela	Hold tight, *Favela,*
que as coisas vão melhorar.	things are gonna get better.

—Benedita da Silva

Let me take you on a little tour of Chapéu Mangueira, where I have been living all my life. In Brazil, we call these poor neighborhoods *favelas,* which I suppose you would translate as slums. Chapéu Mangueira is considered a very small *favela,* with only about 2,000 inhabitants. Like most *favelas* in Rio, it's perched on a hillside. There are no paved roads and cars can't come up here. The few people who have cars park them down below and then walk up.

Tourists who visit the Copacabana beach would never know that there is a *favela* just minutes away. Two blocks from the beach is little alley called Ari Barroso, with a square where the local children play soccer. This is where the *favela* begins. If you walk up the stairs and continue along the dirt path, you'll see what the typical *favela* houses look like. Most of them have just two rooms, with about six people living there, and the houses themselves are not very sturdy. There's no sewage system and no regular garbage collection, which is why you can see a lot of garbage around.

To foreigners the conditions here might look terrible, but things in Chapéu Mangueira are actually much better than in most *favelas.* At least here we have running water, and we have a health clinic and an elementary school. It is also a small *favela,* so there is still a sense of community. People sit outside and talk with their neighbors. The kids are out playing, climbing on the trees. If someone gets sick, people rush to help. My neighbors are always coming to my house to chat, to borrow a cup of sugar, or to tell me about their problems.

The history of the *favelas* goes back to the *quilombos* where the blacks, Indians and some poor whites formed independent republics in the hillsides as a way to resist slavery. The *favelas* are also a result of the rural exodus, with people streaming out of the countryside to the city in search of a better life—just like my parents did. These rural folk, mostly small farmers and their families, are expelled from the land by the big landowners or are already landless and have no way to survive. So they come to the city, look for a piece of empty land, and then occupy it and set up their shacks. Little by little, others join them and form communities. There are now about 480 *favelas* in Rio, which are home to some 2.5 million people.

Most *favelas* in Rio grew up on the hillsides because that's where the empty land was. In addition to the danger of living on steep slopes, we also have to contend with constant struggles over property rights. The struggle around land—with land occupations and conflicts between poor urban dwellers and wealthy landowners—has been a permanent feature of urban life in Rio. After years of fighting for land rights, just 30 percent of *favela* dwellers in this city have legal title to their property.

You have to remember that the *favelas* grew—and continue to grow—out of poverty. No one lives in these neighborhoods because they're nice places to live, but because they have no choice. In many *favelas* conditions are terrible. There's no water, no electricity, no sanitation, and people live crowded on top of each other.

Look at Rocinha, which, ironically, is located in the southern part of the city where Rio's elite live. It's the largest slum in Latin

America and probably in the world. This community of over 200,000 is made up mainly of poor, defenseless, humble people. They don't get any government help, they have no infrastructure or public services such as sewage, water and electricity.

Conditions in Chapéu Mangueira are different because we've had a strong neighborhood association that's been fighting for years to improve the living conditions. I've been working with the association since the time I was 16. I've been president of the association two times. During all these years, we've managed to turn Chapéu Mangueira into a model *favela*. Look at the houses. They have poor sanitation and people are crowded together, but about 95 percent of the houses are made of brick. In other *favelas* you'll see houses made of everything—plywood, stucco, tin, even cardboard. And here we all have running water and electricity in our homes.

Through the neighborhood association, we've managed to get a lot of services for the community. Here on the right is the health center we built. It includes preventive medicine, pediatrics, prenatal care, and special services for seniors and adolescents. We offer dental assistance with services like filling cavities, making crowns and false teeth, and applying fluoride.

This building next to the clinic is our elementary school. We fought hard to get this school in our community, because it makes it so much easier for the children to attend school. And over there, that building under construction, that's going to be our daycare center. Unfortunately, we've had to stop work on it because we don't have enough money to finish it. The daycare center is my pet project—it's my baby. I've been dreaming of having a daycare center here for years. We received some donations from churches to start it, but we still need more money. My idea is to use the profits from this book to fund the rest of it. It will be so wonderful to have a decent place for the little ones to play—something I never had as a child.

If you look up there to the top of the hill, you'll see our water tank. We all helped build that tank, carrying the stones and cement up the hill on our heads—men, women, children, everyone. Most of what we've done here has been thanks to our own labor. The government did almost nothing, and when it did get involved it was mainly to fight with us. In 1968 we asked the government for help in shoring up the slopes of the hill, but we had to wait until 1995—27 years—for them to start!

We're proud that we did everything ourselves, but today we're starting to question whether that's the way it should be. We're aware that our government has the duty to use our taxes to improve our community. No one asks the people who live along the plush Vieira Souto to go out on Saturdays and Sundays and join work brigades!

Now we have an agreement with the state to pay the people who work in the clinic and the school, but before they were all volunteers and the community had to pay for all the materials. We still do all kinds of fund-raisers to fund our projects—parties, cultural events and sending proposals abroad. We've had some help from Canada and from some local churches. But most of this should be the government's responsibility.

You see that small store front over there? That's the *birosca*, where they sell a little bit of this, a little bit of that. Notice the young girl helping her mother mind the store. She's only about seven years old. It's very common in the *favelas* to see children working. The children help their parents with the household chores, and they also help earn money. Nowadays most of them also go to school, so they have little time to play. I know they have to help their parents make money but it would be so much nicer if they could just go to school and play. They have almost no childhood because they have to take on so many responsibilities.

Poor Brazilians begin working at a very early age. That's why we're trying to change the law so that people can retire after a certain number of years of service instead of at a certain age.

Over there are the garbage bins. They're collected once a week, but as you can see, they're already overflowing. There aren't enough bins and the garbage isn't collected often enough. People are also not very conscious about sanitation; some people throw their garbage right in the street or in back of their houses. We're trying to educate the community more about sanitation and also to implement a recycling program, but it's a slow process.

One thing that people in the *favela* are really conscious about is preserving the trees and plants. We try to keep as much of the greenery as we can. When we build our houses, we build around the trees. Look at all this beautiful greenery—we have wonderful fruit trees, like mango and *jaca*. It gives the community a rural flavor, even though we're in the middle of the city.

I used to climb these trees when I was a child. We'd tie ropes from one to another to make our own swings, and we'd play hopscotch here in the street. That's because when we tried to play in the public squares people would chase us away. "Only children can play here," they'd say. Poor children weren't even considered children; they only wanted children accompanied by their nannies.

Over here is the meeting place for the neighborhood committee. It looks like just another house, but it's really our community center. Unfortunately, I don't go to community meetings very often anymore. My friends expect me to go but I just don't have the time. They come to me when there are problems, though, and I try to help out. Right now there's a problem with the water that I'm trying to get fixed. I also participate in cultural events, like organizing a carnival group to commemorate the abolition of slavery.

We have lots of cultural events in the community center. Right now there's a theater group in there practicing a play. It's important to do cultural work with the young people because through art they can explore their creativity and their leadership abilities. It's an opportunity for them to participate in a project they can be proud of. That's why we promote theater groups and samba groups.

That guy I just said hello to, he's a wonderful musician and he's involved with one of the *escolas de samba,* the big samba groups. We were just commenting on how sad it is that carnival has become so commercial and has lost its roots. Carnival really started to change for the worse when the middle class got involved. First of all, it became intellectualized. Today the samba groups are not judged by the community itself but by a commission that uses academic standards to analyze the rhythm and the rhyme.

Another change is that they are now so extravagant and commercialized. The *sambista* that dances in the front with the *bateria,* the drummers, is not necessarily the best dancer but the one who is young and beautiful and has the prettiest legs. Groups like Império Serrano that have maintained their traditions have suffered—they don't win awards because they don't fit into the new criteria. The most popular samba group in Rio today is called Mangueira, but my favorite is Salgueiro, which is one of the more traditional groups.

It's just like in soccer—the most popular team is Flamengo, but I like Botafogo better. What can I say? I've always liked them because they're a team that recruits poor, black players. So many kids in the *favelas* dream of being soccer players, but they don't have many opportunities because the soccer schools are for middle class kids who can afford them. But Botafogo is trying to change this. It doesn't have big name players on the team, but is has a lot of soul.

I'm such a Botafogo fan that it has been really nerve-racking for me to watch these last few games. It was the first time in 20 years that Botafogo had a chance to win the national championship, and the suspense was too much for me. When the final game between Botafogo from Rio and Santos from São Paulo took place last week, I was flying between Brasília and Rio. I purposely took that flight so I wouldn't have to watch the game and suffer through it. I even took a Walkman with me to listen to music and distract myself. I didn't want to hear the score until it was over. But halfway through the game, the pilot got on the loudspeaker that Botafogo was winning 1 to 0.

I was thrilled, but soon after he announced tha tied and that was too much for me. I couldn't stand it. I called the flight attendant to see if he could ask the pilot to stop talking about the game until we landed. When we got to Rio, the streets were already full of people celebrating because Botafogo had won. I went home and watched a tape of the game on television and the next day I went to the Botafogo headquarters to celebrate with them. Everyone was dancing and singing and cheering—we had such a fabulous time. After all, we'd waited 20 years for this!

In our organizing work with youth in the *favela,* sports are very important. These kids don't have money to join sports clubs and get formal training. Here in Chapéu Mangueira, the neighborhood association uses sports and cultural activities to help the kids develop their creativity. Whether it's a sports team, a theater club or samba group, it's a chance for young people to work together and to develop their self-esteem. It's also a way to keep the kids out of trouble.

I'm in favor of all kinds of cultural expressions. One of the most popular cultural expressions in the *favela* today is funk music. Down in the square at the entrance to the *favela,* just below my house, the kids have had funk dances every Friday night with DJs playing loud music. The dances used to last until four or five in the morning until the neighbors started to complain, so now they end earlier.

Funk music and dance is exploding in the *favelas,* and it's not just attracting poor kids, but middle class kids as well. I'd say that 80 percent of the youth at the dances are middle class kids slumming it in the *favelas.* You see them come here in their cars or fancy motorcycles. Some people think that funk is associated with delinquency and encourage the police to ban funk dances. A lot of the better-off parents don't like their kids going to the *favelas.* I remember a letter a mother wrote to the newspaper complaining that thanks to funk, "my children now think that poverty is beautiful and that the *favelas* are wonderful places." But I think it's really healthy to bring the youth of different classes together.

The more we understand each other's realities, the better. When outsiders come to the *favela* and meet people here, they realize that most of us are hard-working people who, if given a chance, could do a lot to improve our community. You see that guy over there building another room on top of his house? People here have the skills to build good houses, they just don't have the financial means. We're the ones who build the houses where the rich live, so we know how to do it. When houses in the *favela* collapse it's not because they're poorly built but because they're made out of cheap material.

My first house was a small one-room shack. The roof was made out of old tin cans, and the walls were made from wooden boxes. The second was more sophisticated—it was made of old pieces of wood left over from construction sites. When it leaked, we'd fill the holes with rags. The third house was made of wood and bamboo that we covered with clay and then whitewashed. Today I have a house made out of brick.

It took me 15 years to build the house I live in today. I designed it myself and I'm very proud of how beautiful it is. Everyone in the family worked on it—men, women, and children. Some say it's a bourgeois house because it has three bedrooms, a living room, a kitchen, a bathroom and a verandah. If that's what they call bourgeois, then I wish everyone could have a bourgeois house.

Providing decent housing should be a national priority, but instead the government is cutting public investment for urban projects and low-income housing. So people have no alternative but to continue to stream into the *favelas,* and build shacks on the banks of rivers and dangerous hillsides.

From the time the *favelas* first appeared, we've had to rely on our own organizing efforts to get anything done. I started working in our community organization here in Chapéu Mangueira from the time I was a teenager. I worked with a group of women to teach other women and children in the neighborhood how to read and write. I wasn't trained as a teacher and we didn't have a formal school for giving classes. We started out using a space in the church, then we used a room in the health clinic. It wasn't until years later that we managed to build our own elementary school.

While this literacy work was useful, many of us felt the need to create an organization that would work to improve the basic living conditions in the *favela*. With the support of the Catholic Church, we started organizing committees to work on issues like housing, electricity, health and education. For example, tuberculosis was a very serious health problem and, with the help of a Dominican nun named René, we started a health campaign that virtually eradicated tuberculosis.

The government never helped us; in fact, it considered the *favelas* illegal communities and felt threatened by our organizing work. Families would move into the *favelas* during the night and quickly put up their shacks, and during the day the police would come and tear them down. When we tried to get a sewage system put in, they refused to extend the pipes to our community. Can you imagine that? They didn't even want the feces of the rich to be contaminated by the feces of the poor!

In the 1950s, these neighborhood committees were cropping up all over the *favelas* to push for our basic rights. The government decided that the best way to try to control these groups would be to take them over. So they created government-run neighborhood associations in the *favelas* where they dictated the rules and regulations and tried to co-opt the local leaders. But most of us understood what the government was trying to do, and we resisted. We took back the associations and put them under popular control, and then we created the Federation of *Favelas* to group all the associations together. This way we were able to gain more power to pressure the government to meet our demands.

In 1958, when I was 16, I became the secretary of the neighborhood association of Chapéu Mangueira because I was one of the few people in the community who knew how to read and write. As the secretary, I mainly did small administrative tasks and things like serving coffee to the leaders. Later I worked on the committee that was trying to get electricity into the community, and then on the committee in charge of building the water tank. I also helped Sister René in the health clinic and literacy program.

My husband Mansinho would tell me that my community work was dangerous and that I could get arrested because the government would think I was a communist. But he didn't stop me from participating, and I tried to get him more involved by having some of the meetings at our house so he would get to know the people I worked with. He was jealous of my male friends, but I knew how to handle him.

While the government considered the organizers communists, the truth is that the Communist Party didn't have much influence in the *favelas*. Their strength was in the union movement and they didn't see improving the living conditions in the *favelas* as their priority. Even so, the government saw the *favelas* as a hotbed of subversives, and when the military coup took place in 1964, they unleashed a massive wave of repression against us. Many *favelas* were physically destroyed. The military would come in and raze whole neighborhoods. Then they'd move the people to remote areas that were far from where they worked. It was difficult for children to get to their schools. Women who did laundry for a living lost their jobs because there was no room to wash clothes in the new neighborhoods. Men would often start second families because they were unable to return home after work every day.

Those who managed to remain in the *favelas* were targets of repression. The army invaded our neighborhoods and destroyed our

Outcomes from Government repression

shacks using any pretext they could find—a fight in the family, an illegal addition on a house, things like that. If our roofs were falling apart we weren't allowed to fix them. They wanted our houses to collapse so we'd abandon them and move away. We weren't allowed to expand our houses or build new houses. So the *favelas* began to grow vertically as a way to get around the restrictions.

People didn't get married because they weren't allowed to build new houses. That's when we started to see more pregnant girls, more prostitution, and a general breakdown in social relations. It was a difficult period, not only economically but from an ethical and moral standpoint as well.

The repression touched every part of our lives. We didn't have the same visibility as the intellectuals or middle class activists who went abroad into exile. We were exiled in our own country. We weren't allowed to sing our religious hymns or celebrate our festivals. We dug holes in our houses to hide our books and notepads. We couldn't keep minutes of our meetings because it was considered subversive to demand better living conditions like electricity, plumbing or paved roads.

Some community organizers had to leave home and go into hiding. Many people were arrested, including my second husband Bola. He was coming out of a meeting one night when the police came and rounded everyone up. Luckily, they didn't find any evidence against Bola because we managed to hide his notes and books. Eventually they let him go.

Because I was a woman, I was never arrested or put in jail. But the officials in charge of controlling the community knew that I was one of the leaders of the neighborhood association, and they tried to make my life miserable. They would spread lies about me to discredit me and create divisions among us.

They also tried to use our own children to spy on us. Children who gave messages and information to the military were called *aviõezinhos,* or little airplanes. The army would come up to the *favelas* and ask the children where the meetings were taking place, who attended them, what they discussed or where the people they were looking for were hiding. The children often heard their parents talk about something and would innocently pass the information on. Many of their mothers did the laundry for those in power or for the soldiers, and it was the children who would collect the laundry and deliver it. So when they went to their houses to pick up the wash, they'd be interrogated. I know this for a fact because my own children and my neighbors' children were used that way.

In later years, during the 1980s, the children went on to be used by organized crime, which became more sophisticated during the dictatorship. And today the children of the poor are used as informers for the drug traffickers.

There were not many avenues open for us to organize during the dictatorship, but I started to work with the Catholic Church and with the underground left parties that organized in the *favelas* through literacy programs. We began a literacy campaign here in Chapéu Mangueira and used methods developed by the great educator Paulo Freire, which not only taught people to read, but raised their consciousness at the same time. It was a highly revolutionary way of teaching compared to the official teaching methods, which were very traditional. Brazilian education assumed that there were no inequalities in our society, that there was no class or ethnic consciousness.

Our method for teaching people to read and write was based on relating everything to their everyday lives. For example, instead of using a standard teaching phrase like *"o Ivo vê a uva,"* Ivan sees the grape, we'd say *"o Ivo vê a vala,"* Ivan sees the ditch. Or take the standard phrase *"o gato bebeu o leite do prato,"* the cat drank milk from the plate. We couldn't use that because in the *favela* people didn't have cats as pets—we ate them. Cat was the poor man's meat. It was a feast when you could kill a nice, fat cat.

So instead we used phrases like *"o morro não tem água,"* the neighborhood doesn't have water—because back then it didn't. That's what our lessons were like and this was our subtle way of doing political work during the dictatorship.

One of the positive changes that happened during the dictatorship was that the women's movement in the *favelas* gained strength. Before the coup, women played a backstage role within the neighborhood associations. We would usually do the administrative work, make the food for the parties, and work on health and education. But when it came to decision-making, the men were in charge.

During the years of military rule, women were forced to take over many of their roles since the men in the *favelas* who were community organizers were persecuted. Many women leaders, myself included, emerged during this period. I became so active that in 1978 the women put me forward as a candidate for president of our association, and I won. It was a first for Chapéu Mangueira.

Since the dictatorship we've accomplished a lot through our organizing work here in the *favela*. But now we have another terrible problem to contend with—the invasion of drugs in our community. There were no drugs in the *favelas* when I was growing up. Now everything has changed. There are some *favelas* that are completely controlled by the drug dealers.

It's very painful for me to see the influence of drugs right here in my own community. The majority of these young people involved in drugs are sons of my friends and colleagues of my children. I try to work with them—both politically and spiritually—whenever I can. I try to get scholarships for them to study because you can't go to them empty-handed. You have to offer some other prospect that might be attractive to them. If they don't have jobs or schools to go to, if there's no alternative, they'll always go back to drugs and crime. But I know that deep down, they really don't want to be involved in drugs. I've never heard a boy say, "When I grow up, I want to be a big drug dealer."

We don't have many drug addicts because people in the *favelas* are too poor to be big consumers of drugs. The consumers come mainly from the better-off neighborhoods to buy their drugs in the *favelas*. And the drug dealers in the *favelas* usually don't commit crimes against their neighbors. They have their own code, their own rules that say they shouldn't bother their neighbors so as not to attract the police. In fact, the people in the *favelas* are usually more afraid of the police than the drug dealers. The police are suspicious of everyone because they think the neighbors are covering up for the drug dealers.

The worst thing about the drugs is the clashes it brings between the dealers and the police. Many innocent people in Chapéu Mangueira have died in these conflicts. In 1990 there was a horrible massacre right in front of my house. One afternoon I heard my neighbor, Maria Helena, screaming, and I ran outside to see what happened. Her 22-year-old son Aguinaldo had been shot as he was walking up the steps to the *favela*. Aguinaldo was such a nice boy, he was in the Navy and had nothing to do with drugs; he was just an innocent bystander. Maria Helena ran to help him, and then she, too, was gunned down. So was Damião, a young 19-year-old boy who sold flowers in the market. All three of them died.

The killers belonged to a hit squad made up of members of the police force. It seems they had come to find a boy who knew that the police were getting kickbacks from the drug dealers. They came in plain clothes, in an unmarked car, shooting wildly. They call this *"queima de arquivo,"* burn the archive, because the boy they were looking for was a police informer.

I didn't know who they were and I ran to the police station for help, but no one was there. Two hours later, more than 10 police cars showed up and when they got near the scene of the massacre one of the drug dealers yelled, "Benedita, the one who did this is a cop called 'Thirty Dollars.' " I felt like *o cocô do cavalo do bandido* — a horse's ass. I had called the police for help and then I realized that it was the police themselves who'd been responsible for the killing. I thought it was my duty to call the police, but I learned a bitter lesson. That was the last time I ever asked the police to come into the *favela*.

In some *favelas* the drug dealers get community support because they perform a lot of services that should be performed by the government. They pay for schools, burials, birthday parties, baptisms, Christmas celebrations. They play the role of the state and godfather wrapped in one. That's why there's a certain idealization of the anti-hero of the *favela* who uses drug money to provide assistance to the community.

Chapéu Mangueira is one of the places that has most resisted the influence of the traffickers. Our neighborhood association refuses to accept drug money. When the dealers offer to help with one thing or another, the neighbors say, "We don't need your help. Benedita will take care of it for us." That's why I go crazy when I can't solve a problem in the neighborhood. In other *favelas* where there's not a strong community organization, it becomes very easy for the dealers to take hold.

The drugs and violence have turned Rio into an urban prison. I'm not just talking about the *favelas,* but the rich parts of town as well. Security systems, condominiums with guards, remote control gates, attack dogs, and bodyguards have become indispensable for the "tranquillity" of the rich. Even their children grow up with tremendous paranoia—locked in, surrounded by guards, afraid of being kidnapped.

The rich blame the *favelas* for the climate of violence. They talk about the need to remove the *favelas* that are too close to the nice parts of town. But here in the *favelas* the people realize that the drug dealers and criminals in the neighborhood are a small slice of a big business that moves millions of dollars. We know that these dealers and thieves are the "small fries"—they don't have economic power or political clout. The true sharks, the bosses, don't live in the *favelas*. They're the ones who profit the most but take the least risks. The big guys take advantage of the misery in the *favela* to make their profits. Crime and delinquency don't come down from the *favela* to contaminate the rest of the city. On the contrary, they come from the rich parts of town and make their way up to the *favela*. The *favela* is violated, invaded, used.

Putting an end to urban violence means seeking out the big-time criminals wherever they are, and cutting off their ties with the *favelas*. Putting an end to urban violence means putting an end to the speculation and greed of those who control the profits. Putting an end to violence means giving people in the countryside a piece of land so that they have a way to feed themselves. It means adequate schools so that everyone can get a decent education. It means generating jobs with livable wages.

It's clear that there are no magical solutions to the problems in the *favelas*. But there is a fundamental principle that must be respected: The people must be allowed to remain in their communities. The solution is not to move them elsewhere but to improve living conditions in the *favelas*.

First of all, people must be given title to the land so they can have more security. There must be infrastructure projects that use the work force that is so plentiful in the *favelas*. Families who now live in dangerous places—on the slopes or the banks of rivers— must be relocated. The *favelas* must have their own schools, health clinics, cultural centers, and training programs that can give young people the skills they need to find jobs.

Today there are some 35 million slum dwellers in Brazil. With just three percent of the GNP, all the *favelas* of Brazil could be urbanized in five years, giving them schools, daycare centers, clinics, paved roads, brick houses, electricity, water and sewage systems. But the only way we're going to get the government to listen to us and to devote funds to the *favelas* is through organizing. Only organized communities can successfully make demands and influence government decisions. If they are not organized, they remain totally isolated and marginalized. Those of us who live in the *favelas* must strengthen our neighborhood associations, our political parties that are fighting on behalf of the poor, our unions, our religious organizations, or any other grouping that can stand up for our rights. That's the only way to have political clout.

I'm an example of a grassroots leader who was born out of organizing in the *favelas*. After I was first elected to the City Council in 1982, my comrades were so proud! They had seen me going up and down the road to the *favela* endless times, lugging bags of laundry for my mother to wash or balancing buckets of water on my head.

After the election, I went to the market in my slippers one day and when I got back home my neighbors in the association said, "Can we ask you something? Please don't go out again in your slippers. Remember, you're a councilwoman now." The truth is that people who live in the *favelas* don't like to look or dress like poor people. The artist Joãozinho Trinta says that the only ones who like poverty are intellectuals, and he's right.

My neighbors convinced me to buy a car because they didn't want me to keep walking up to the *favela* on foot. They'll soon be telling me that I should buy a house in a nice neighborhood and leave the *favela*. Some people are already saying that it's dangerous for me to stay, that there's no security here.

But I love my house and so far, even Pitanga hasn't convinced me to leave. He tells me, "I married you, my love, to take you away from the *favela* and instead you brought me here." Pitanga is from the middle class, but he came to live with me in the *favela* out of love. I'm sure that I'll leave one day, but I still have a hard time getting used to the idea. I still have to be close to my community, fighting to make more improvements. My son, my sisters, my nephews—they're all here. My whole family lives in the *favela,* the only one who left is my daughter, but that was just recently. I'm not in a hurry to leave here.

One of the things I'd miss most is the view. We can't finish this tour without going up to the top of the hill so you can see the fantastic view we have of Rio. . . .

From up here you can see the whole Copacabana beach, with the beautiful mountains in the background. It looks like a postcard, doesn't it? Rio is a very lovely city. It's also an important economic center—not only for its residents, the *cariocas,* but for the whole country.

The people who come down from the *favelas* are the ones who supply the cheap labor that builds this marvelous city—its mansions, its high-rises, its luxury restaurants. They are the bricklayers, the plumbers, firefighters, the humble factory workers who help make the profits for the big companies. They are the maids and the waiters, the people who serve the privileged classes. They are hardworking people, people who are proud of their culture. But cast aside by the very people they serve, they can't even enjoy the fruits of their labor. It's a sad contradiction.

Chapter Three
No One Said Politics Would Be Easy

Benedita during her campaign for the Senate

Photo by Jorge Nunes

Política é coisa pra macho	Politics is a man's game
ouvi isso a vida inteira	I heard that all my life
tem que ter sabedoria	You have to be well-educated
experiência voraz	have tons of experience
formado em filosofia	a degree in philosophy
melhor mesmo economia	better yet, economics
ou você não é capaz.	or else you're not competent.
Tem que ter muito dinheiro	You have to have lots of money
ser de família tradicional	come from a traditional family
ouça bem o que te digo	listen carefully to what I say
se você é operário	if you're a worker
não é intelectual	not an intellectual
cai fora desse pedaço	you're out of the running
isso é pra profissional.	this is for professionals
O poder não se divide	Power is never shared
não se dá	nor given away
mas se conquista	power is taken
não é fácil	it's not easy
sempre disse	I always say

—Benedita da Silva

I was very reluctant to run for city council. I was happy with my organizing work in the Chapéu Mangueira neighborhood association, where I was fighting for the rights of women and blacks, and for better living conditions in the *favelas*.

The Workers Party (PT) wanted candidates who had a grass-roots base, and they asked the *favela* associations to come up with a slate of candidates. So we all had meetings to elect our representatives. The people in my association encouraged me to run, especially the women. The idea of going into political life did not really appeal to me. As a political figure I knew I'd be the target of criticism and would be more vulnerable. But I had always been one of the women fighting for women to take on positions of power, so I felt I almost didn't have a choice. The women were so encouraging and supportive that I couldn't let them down.

I was also insecure, and I never thought I'd win. I belonged to a new party, with a new political platform and I was an unknown. Plus, we hardly had money. And when my campaign started, the women did everything to raise money—they sold pastries, they made clothing, all kinds of things.

The bulk of my campaign was spent in the street asking people to vote for me. I'd take a box and go to the public squares where there were a lot of housewives, and I'd get up on the box and start talking to them. I'd go from neighborhood to neighborhood, even from door to door. Unlike the rest of the candidates, I couldn't afford to print posters and couldn't even rent a car with loud speakers. I had the right to free TV time, but I didn't have money to pay the production costs. It was only in the last week of the campaign that I could rent studio time and produce a TV spot.

While I felt okay talking to people from my own social class, sometimes I'd be invited to meetings at fancy places full of "ologists"—sociologists, anthropologists, psychologists—and I'd get all nervous and shy. At one event, I was very quiet until I heard a woman say that the only way to solve the problem of the *favelas* was to tear them down and send the people to live on the outskirts of the city. I couldn't keep my mouth shut; I had to respond. I said that I was sure that her maid lived in a *favela* and that if she had to move far away, she wouldn't get to work on time to take care of this woman's children and clean her house. I said that instead of tearing down the *favelas,* we had to improve the living conditions there. I realized that I was one of the few people running for office who had firsthand experience living in a *favela*.

I was one of the few representatives of the neighborhood associations to become a candidate, and the first woman. It was a tremendous responsibility. Some people said I was charismatic, but the truth is that I never thought I'd be elected.

I was elected with more votes than any other council person in Rio. I couldn't believe it!

I was even more terrified after I won. I thought that I'd have the support of others in the Party, but I was the only PT member in Rio elected to the city council. Once again, it was the women who came to my aid, who gave me support and advice. A very important woman in my life at that time was Hildezia Alves. She was a professor and became one of my political advisers. She was a black woman, and a great activist.

Hildezia began to work with me in 1983, helping me overcome my fears, my lack of experience, my contradictions. She taught me how to have patience, how to deal with sexism within my own team, and how to take charge when my tendency was to pull back.

She also helped me figure out how to reconcile my personal relationship with Bola with our political work.

In the beginning, I was afraid of the whole legislative process, all the formal procedures and the fancy vocabulary. I always enjoyed studying, that wasn't the problem. I was coming from a grassroots base and this new forum was so elitist. I hated spending hours and hours in meetings. I was used to working directly with the community—pulling up our sleeves, getting everyone together, and solving the problems. Sometimes I'd be sitting in these interminable meetings and I'd feel like getting up and leaving, and never coming back.

I also had to confront differences with my own party, the Workers Party. I didn't want to identify with any particular tendency, and I felt isolated. Since I was the only elected representative, I thought that the party leadership would use my position as a springboard to develop its work in Rio. But the party didn't understand that my position really belonged to them, and didn't make good use of the access I had gained. Since the party was so new, it was having a difficult time dealing with power, and understanding the relationship between its elected officials and the grassroots base.

Luckily, I had help from a good team. Hildezia, for one, understood what was going on and she'd say, "Let's do what you were elected to do, let's get the work done. The Workers Party is still new. You were elected to represent the party and they will have to understand that."

I also had help from two important men. One was Hermogenes de Almeida, a black friend who devoted a lot of time to me. This kind of help from men was not common because most men in the party opted to work in the campaigns of other men. But Hermogenes was very special.

When we had already picked the Workers Party candidates for the 1982 elections and were deciding who would work with whom, he stood up at the meeting and said, "I want to support the women and work on the campaign of Benedita da Silva." He was the one who wrote my first campaign material. He helped me with everything—from writing and designing the literature to mapping out the political strategies. We saw eye-to-eye on a lot of things, and we also had some good fights!

Hermogenes was the one who introduced me to the black movement in Brazil. He was also the one who defended me when people criticized me for being Evangelical, because in those days the black movement was trying to promote Afro-Brazilian religions and they saw the Evangelical Church as a non-black religion.

Unfortunately, Hermogenes was murdered a few years later on the night of June 14, 1994. He was 39 years old. I remember that night as if it were yesterday. That day we had participated in a seminar against police violence. That same night, when he was leaving a party, he was shot in cold blood. It was a senseless, random shooting. I couldn't believe it. I was devastated. . . . Hermogenes was a writer, an intellectual, and a totally marvelous person. It was a tragedy and a cruel twist of fate.

When I was elected to the city council, I also received a great deal of support from my husband Bola, who ran my office. Working together helped us combine our political work and our personal lives. I knew how important this was, because I've always had to juggle different facets of my life, like when I was president of the Chapéu Mangueira neighborhood association and also ran a household, worked, and studied at the same time.

We had all kinds of people working in my office—blacks, whites, people from the *favela,* intellectuals. It was incredibly diversified and that was critical for my learning. I've always had the humility to recognize my limits and this has helped me learn from others.

At first I felt that the other city council members treated me with a certain degree of paternalism and tokenism. Some were outright racist. I heard people talking about me, calling me *"neguinha do morro,"* little nigger from the hills, and insinuating that

I was illiterate and incompetent. This attitude started to change once I began to make speeches and present my proposals.

I stirred up quite a lot of controversy in the council because I insisted that we had to guarantee a space for the voice of the community, rich and poor. One highly controversial project I introduced was called *Tribuna Popular.* I proposed that community leaders be allowed to meet with city council members on a regular basis and participate in our discussions. Although the community representatives wouldn't have the right to vote, the majority of council members didn't support the idea because they considered themselves to be the true representatives of the people and this would undermine their authority. I was never able to get the project approved.

I introduced other controversial projects such as one called Neighborhood Rights, which limited the construction of high-rises in the city. I also wanted to introduce building codes that would be beneficial to domestic workers. People build enormous apartments but make the maid's room a little box. That's how I started to work for the rights of domestic workers.

I also fought for the preservation of the Copacabana Palace, a beautiful hotel along the beach that was a favorite hangout for the Brazilian elite and foreign visitors. I voted for the hotel to be designated an historic landmark. I always had a broad vision and knew that I should work for all people — both rich and poor. While my primary interest was with the poor, I understood that I was supposed to represent the interests of all social classes, that all people who paid taxes deserved my attention.

My election to the city council was only possible because of the creation of the Workers Party in the last years of the dictatorship. During the dictatorship, only two political parties were allowed — the National Renovation Alliance (ARENA) and the Brazilian Democratic Movement (MDB). ARENA was the pro-government party. Like most people in the popular movement, I supported the MDB. But in the case of both parties, the politicians would come to the *favela,* give speeches and leave, while we just sat there and listened.

The workers in the union movement also realized that the traditional parties didn't represent them. The turning point for the creation of a new party came in 1979, at a meeting of metalworkers, mechanics, and electricians in São Paulo. The participants, who represented more than a million workers, voted to form the Workers Party. Right after that, they started distributing their statement of principles, and seeking allies within the popular movements. The Workers Party, which became known by its initials PT, was officially launched in February 1980.

Until the appearance of the PT, political life in Brazil had been totally controlled by powerful economic interests. The military government did what it could to stop the PT's growth. Party offices were burglarized and burned, activists in several parts of the country were arrested. But despite the repression, the party continued to grow not only among workers, but among other sectors of society.

The PT understood the need to be as broad-based as possible. The progressive wing of the Catholic church supported the formation of the PT, and the religious workers in the *favelas* brought us materials and information about the new party. The ideas that the PT represented resonated with my own beliefs, and I became a strong supporter. We would go door to door in the *favelas,* explaining what the party was about and recruiting new members.

I wanted to create support for the party within the leadership of the Federation of *Favelas.* A few community leaders didn't want to get involved with the PT. They were members of the Communist Party before the dictatorship crushed it, and thought of the PT as a party of *igrejeiros* — church-goers. But little by little I convinced them to work with us.

I was always religious, and even though I believed in socialism,

I couldn't identify with other left-wing parties because they were atheist. But the PT was different. It welcomed both atheists and believers. It reached out to intellectuals and grassroots organizers. It also promised new opportunities for women.

In the beginning, it was often difficult for people like myself, who came from the grassroots, to find a voice within the party. The intellectuals in the party used a language that was very different from ours. But for that reason, it was like a big school for all of us. The debates between the different sectors expanded our political horizons and led to critical discussions of issues around class, race, and gender. In spite of the internal divisions, I think these debates were healthy for the party's political growth, because they allowed an open forum for discussing issues from different perspectives. Today, the PT has all kinds of elected officials, from factory workers to intellectuals.

There are wonderful people in the PT, but I must confess that my number one love is Luis Inácio Lula da Silva. Lula came from a family of poor peasants, who left their land in the northeast and came to São Paulo in search of a better life. The happiest moment of his mother's life was when Lula landed a job as a metal-worker—she died before she could see him become a creator of the nation's largest federation of unions and a founder of the Workers Party. Lula was so charismatic that he became the PT presidential candidate in 1989 and lost the presidency by a mere three percent of the votes.

The internal diversity in the Workers Party is a credit to Lula's vision and audacity. As we women say, Lula was the one who "sewed" the party together. Sometimes, when I get discouraged with politics, I remember that it was Lula who put oil in this machine and we can't let it break down. When I'm stressed out and think about dropping my political work, I think of Lula and feel ashamed to even consider giving up.

I'm so proud of Lula, and I love him very much. It's a sisterly kind of love. Pitanga knows I'm crazy about Lula, so does Lula's wife Mariza. Lula reminds me of my second husband Bola. Some people think I have a crush on him but even if I laid in bed with Lula, nothing would happen.

I love Lula because he is so smart and sensitive. His rich and powerful political opponents had to resort to dirty tricks to stop him from being elected president. They pressured his first wife to say that Lula had forced her to have an abortion, which is illegal in Brazil. It was a total lie, because his wife never had an abortion and Lula has a wonderful relationship with his daughter. And to discredit him even more right before the vote, the major TV news program showed its tremendous bias by editing the last presidential debate to highlight Lula's weaknesses and the strengths of his opponent Fernando Collor. Despite the low blows, in 1989 he received over 30 million votes.

Lula has been a great inspiration to me. He has always played a mediating role in the PT and he realizes the importance of working at the grassroots level. After his second attempt at the presidency in 1994, he decided to step down as top leader of the party and instead devote himself to strengthening the party's base.

Lula has always paid attention to women's demands. He was even open to our criticism of his personal life when we suggested that his wife, Mariza, play a greater role in his presidential campaign. In spite of Lula's openness, we women had to fight hard to gain leadership positions in the PT. Though we were always behind the scenes doing the work, very few women were chosen by the party to run for office. Today, at least 30 percent of the leadership positions must be held by women. This was something we fought for within the party and won.

It wasn't easy to establish this 30 percent quota for women in the party. Some men insisted that there was no gender discrimination in the party and that women could become leaders once we proved our competency. We said, "What are you talking about?

We've already proven our competency by doing all kinds of work in the PT, we're just not getting the recognition." We had to convince them that the quota was necessary because discrimination was the real reason we were not in leadership positions.

We women make other demands on the men in the party. For example, we insist that PT leaders pay child support. We've already vetoed the candidacy of some men who want to defend the rights of working people but won't give financial support to their children. They get furious, but it forces them to confront their contradictions. How can a person be trusted to defend the rights of children if he won't even take care of his own children?

We know that sexism doesn't exist only in the PT. It exists in all parties, it exists throughout the entire society. Everywhere there are men and women working together there's going to be some degree of sexism, just like everywhere that blacks and whites are working together there's going to be some degree of racism. It's something that all of us — women, men, blacks, whites — have to struggle against.

I confront racism and sexism every day of my life, so I know how critical it is to constantly fight against discrimination. People call me ugly and a monkey. They tell me to go pick bananas and to go back to the kitchen. I receive racist and sexist letters written on toilet paper. And now that I'm more vocal about these issues and more well known, I'm attacked more than ever.

There is a stereotype of who can be intelligent and competent, who can have power. In Brazil it is rich, white men who represent the face of power. My opponent during the mayoral race took advantage of that. He'd say, "Are you intelligent? Are you a winner? Then vote for me." People want to identify themselves with the winners.

That's why so many people fail to vote for the candidates who really represent their interests. It would be very cruel of me to berate the poor for not voting for other poor people, or blacks for not voting for other blacks, women for women, workers for workers. But what's important is to analyze why people tend to discredit candidates who are similar to themselves.

During my recent campaign, I remember two women factory workers looked at me in disgust and threw my pamphlet on the ground. I picked it up, handed it back to them and said, "Hello. I'm Benedita da Silva, candidate for federal deputy. I'm a woman just like you. I'm a worker."

If poor and black women always see themselves portrayed as losers, their dream is to be like Xuxa, the big TV star who has a show for kids. Xuxa has everything—she's young, blond and pretty and gets paid millions of dollars for playing with kids.

There were even women who didn't support a national campaign we launched to demand that as of 1996, all political parties have at least 20 percent representation by women candidates. These women parroted the same arguments men did—that women should gain leadership positions through their own hard work. They didn't understand that things just don't work that way. We need formal mechanisms to make sure that certain sectors of society—women, blacks, poor people—are valued and recognized.

I'm not saying that people should vote for a candidate only because she's a woman; they should vote for a candidate who will struggle for social justice. But it's more likely that people who have suffered in their lives because of race, gender or class discrimination will be sensitive to the needs of others like them.

A major stumbling block for women and poor people running for office is how to get money to run campaigns. It's easier for me now that I'm well known, but I still have great difficulty. I fund-raise among my friends because I don't get money from big businesses.

I always visit different communities so I can meet people in person. And, of course, if I had more money I could get more votes because I could go to more places. If you're poor and run for office, you have to have a popular base of support. In my case, I have women, blacks, poor, churchgoers, and social activists—these are the people who go out in the streets and help solicit votes for me.

To give you an idea, an average campaign for Senate costs about two million dollars. The well-heeled candidates charter their own airplanes, they pay a lot of staff to work on their campaigns. I don't have anything like that. I spent only about two hundred thousand dollars on my last campaign and I still have an enormous debt to pay off.

Candidates get a certain amount of free air time on radio and TV, but we have to produce our own programs, which is very expensive. And while you're not allowed to buy additional time on the stations, the majority of politicians either have their own radio and TV stations, or they have friends who do. They always find a way to get around the regulations.

A new electoral law also created a special fund to help finance political campaigns. All the parties will receive money from this fund. This is very good for those of us in the PT because the party requires that all its representatives give 30 percent of their salaries to the party. I don't mind giving some kind of contribution, but 30 percent is too much. So this fund will at least help us initiate our campaigns and I hope this means that our contribution to the PT can be reduced.

The government sets limits on the amount of money you can spend on a campaign, but Brazilian elites don't respect the rules and continue to spend fortunes to elect their candidates. It's very common in Brazil to be offered food, employment, school admission, anything in exchange for votes. People blame the poor for selling their votes, but this begins with the elites and is then reproduced at the base of the social pyramid.

The poor sell their votes but it's the rich who buy them. So who corrupts whom? Poor people may vote with their stomachs, but the elites vote to maintain people in power who will help them accumulate their riches—businessmen receive favors, the banks receive greater profits. And as long as there is poverty, the rich will always be able to buy votes.

That's why I think voting should be optional, not mandatory as it is in Brazil today. This would be better for the PT because the people who support us do so consciously. They vote for us because they believe in our political program. We don't buy votes, we don't trade votes for political favors. I think voting should be voluntary, although there are people in the PT who think it's good that it's mandatory. There's no consensus on this in the party.

It was thanks to the consciousness of the voters that I was elected federal deputy for the National Assembly in 1986 and was re-elected four years later. Once again, I never thought I stood a chance of winning. I had almost no TV and radio time. The campaign was mostly me and my supporters getting out and visiting people all over the city. I was encouraged by the fact that wherever I went, huge crowds came out to greet me. My greatest strength is when I get out on the streets and have face-to-face contact with people. Bola and Hermogenes coordinated my first campaign.

Once I was elected deputy, my life changed in all kinds of ways. First of all, I had to move to Brasília, the capital. Bola came to live with me. When we first arrived, we thought we were in another country. We were shocked at how cold a city it was—there were no people walking around in the streets, no human warmth. I also remember that I was very sick with dengue fever. It was horrible. We had to stay in a hotel because although the government provides housing for members of congress, they didn't have an apartment for us yet. So I told them not to worry, that I would find a shack in a poor neighborhood called Taguatinga. I was used to living in the *favela* and thought it would be interesting to have a congressperson living in that community. When the other congressmen found out about my plans, they quickly got me an apartment.

I still haven't gotten used to Brasília. I could never live there for long. I go there during the week to work, and then fly home to Rio on the weekends.

A person who gave me a lot of support during my first years in Congress was Cicera Moraes. She began working with me in 1986. We immediately clicked, and she became responsible for hiring my staff and running the office. Many people don't want to come to Brasília because the salaries for congressional aides are low and the cost of living is very high. But Cicera stayed with me all these years. She's a great worker and a wonderful friend.

Everything changed when I became a congresswoman, including my financial situation. My income leaped tenfold, which I thought was great until I realized that my expenses would be about 20 times more! I have to give 30 percent of my salary to the party, 10 percent to the church I belong to, and I always give another 10 percent to social movements. On top of this, I had to buy a car for the first time in my life, because I couldn't get around by bus anymore. My food costs soared because I couldn't cook and eat at home, and the restaurants in Brasília were so expensive. There are two restaurants in Congress, one I call "Go in poor" and the other "Come out poor." I always eat in the first one.

Another major expense is that now everybody asks for help. I had always shared my poverty with my neighbors. Now that they know I am doing well, they run to me in times of need and, of course, I have to help out.

A surprising increase in my cost of living came from Dona Odete, my dressmaker. As soon as I won the election, she raised her prices fivefold! When I asked her why, she replied, "Deputies have money." It was like that with everyone. Before, when I had a leak in my house, my neighbor would come to fix it. Now he presents his estimate first!

Being in Congress was a major leap in my political responsibilities. I was the first black woman to enter the Congress, and just like when I entered the city council, I was so nervous. I remember my first congressional session when I had to give my opening speech. I wrote the speech over and over again but I was never satisfied. So I decided I would just get up and say whatever came to my mind.

The night before I couldn't sleep a wink. I kept thinking that I was going to do a terrible job, or that people wouldn't pay attention to me. That's why I was so surprised when I walked to the podium and people started applauding. Even more surprising was the silence that took over the room when I began to speak — that's almost unheard of in the Brazilian Congress. People normally keep right on talking while someone else is giving a speech. I'd been thinking that I'd be lucky if I managed to sensitize a handful of the members who were in the first row. But no, the entire plenary stopped talking to listen to me that day.

My speech was a strong indictment of discrimination against blacks and women. I said things like, "If our opinion is not taken into account and we women are not guaranteed equality, we won't feel obligated to respect your laws. We are going to start a rebellion and hundreds of us will occupy the space now taken by insensitive people like you." As you can imagine, these were unusual words in the halls of Congress! But I managed to receive a big round of applause because I was talking genuinely from the heart.

I think that my spontaneous style of speaking gets people's attention. My commitment is not with commas and colons, but with the people. I try not to give typical political speeches because politicians use very formal language.

Sometimes I try to use music and poetry in my speeches. I recently attended an event where we were launching the campaign to get 20 percent representation by women candidates in all the parties. The man who was introducing us asked us not to make long speeches because, he said, women tend to talk too much. We were all really offended. So when it was my turn to talk, instead of bawling him out, I began my speech by singing a song by

Gonzaguinha that says: *"Quando eu soltar a minha voz, por favor entenda, é apenas o meu jeito de dizer o que é amar."* — When I lift my voice to speak please understand, it's just my way of saying what it is to love. It was my way of telling him, in a nice way, that women should be given the chance to talk as long as we like.

We women in Congress have been struggling for years to increase our representation. When I was first elected there were only 26 women out of a total of 599 deputies. It was such a man's world that there still wasn't even a restroom for female deputies. The racial composition was even worse. While 56 percent of Brazilians are black, we were only seven black deputies.

Some people say that the fact that I'm in Congress is proof that there's no discrimination here. I answer that if there were no discrimination I wouldn't be the only black congresswoman in Brazil.

Moreover, congressmen expect women to talk only about women's issues. They tried to stop me from getting involved in discussions about agrarian reform and workers' rights. Women's issues — that was my realm. So I decided to find a way to get around this prejudice of theirs. I would talk about "women and agrarian reform," "women and workers rights," women and everything else, until they finally took me seriously on these issues.

I was always very concerned about being taken seriously. I didn't want to be treated like a token black woman, so I had to be strategic about everything. For example, I love to wear colorful African-type clothing, but when I first started working in the city council and later in Congress, I decided to use a different style. I started out dressing very discreetly, like a good businesswoman. Afterwards, when everyone was used to my presence, I put on my colorful clothes and my African-style braids. By then everyone thought it was very elegant; they didn't see me as just folkloric.

This is part of my strategy. But this doesn't mean that I'm not straightforward in my relationships with people. I maintain my principles, whether it's in the party or at church, whether I'm dealing with whites or blacks, rich or poor. The only thing I might do is change the language I use or my way of approaching each situation.

When I have to confront situations of conflict I first try to find points of common ground and understanding. Of course, I reserve the right to disagree and to fight for my beliefs, but I try not to take our disagreements personally. In politics I have to deal with people from the left, the right, and the center. I put forth my position, and if they don't agree with me, they can vote against me.

I try not to see people as my enemies. To me, the term enemy implies a really cruel hatred, the kind of hatred that makes people kill each other. Yes, there are a lot of people who don't agree with me, and there are people who have a certain jealousy or resentment toward me. I don't try to please everyone, and I'm not an angel. But rather than having enemies, I would say that I have political adversaries.

I also try to maintain my integrity in the face of so much corruption in politics. Actually, no one has ever tried to bribe me; I think my attitude makes people shy away from making illicit proposals. One time, when I was a city councilwoman, a group of lobbyists were pressuring me to vote against designating the Urca Casino as an historical landmark. They sent an old friend of mine, who had helped me in the past, to try to convince me to vote against the bill because they wanted to build a new development on that property. I said I was very sorry, that I would like to help him out, but that I had to vote for what I thought was right, and I voted in favor of the bill. Some politicians get used to asking interest groups for favors, and end up having to sell their souls in return. A friend once told me, "I like you because you always defend your positions, even when it represents a threat to your political career."

It's hard to corrupt me because I learned early in life how to get by on little and I'm not enticed by riches. I eat when there's food and I can go without when there's not. I'm as comfortable going out on the Senate floor as I am climbing up the hill to Chapéu Mangueira. In 1988 when I participated in the celebration of the bicentennial of the Universal Declaration of Human Rights in Paris, a journalist asked me how I felt when I was received in the presidential palace of French President François Mitterrand. I answered, "I felt as comfortable walking into that mansion as I did going up to the *favela* with a bucket of water on my head."

While I deal with many wealthy people, I myself will never accumulate riches, because I always share what I have with others. I don't like to eat in fancy restaurants because I keep thinking that with the same money I could make a feast for my whole family. I only eat in expensive restaurants when someone else is paying. I prefer simple home-made meals, like soup or beans and rice.

My interest in politics is not for personal gain, but to act as a voice for the voiceless. My aim is to help gain access to power for groups that have traditionally been locked out. I don't have any illusion that I'm going to change the entire system, but I can make small gains like helping community radio activists gain access to the airwaves, helping speech-impaired people get sign language in television programming, or helping Afro-Brazilian groups get black history included in the school curricula.

One struggle very close to my heart is for the rights of domestic workers. I fought hard and was able to establish new regulations for this sector, including their right to receive a minimum wage, paid vacations, three months paid maternity leave, and retirement benefits. Recently, I was able to get approval for a number of projects, such as the right of incarcerated women to breast-feed their babies while in jail, a bill that makes it illegal for employers to ask for proof of sterilization for women applying for jobs, and a bill that gives the status of national hero to Zumbi, a leader of the slave rebellion.

Now I'm working on a comprehensive bill to reduce hunger in Brazil. It involves getting the business community and non-governmental organizations to support the creation of small farmers' cooperatives. The bill makes it illegal to store food for the purposes of speculation and makes the government responsible for making sure that sufficient food is available in the internal market. The bill also includes some food distribution, but only in cases of extreme poverty. The main purpose of the project is to increase production, lower prices, and generate employment in the countryside. But I'm running into a lot of opposition on this from the conservative members of Congress.

This is true of all the major projects that the Workers Party supports — agrarian reform and the rights of rural workers, land titles for people living in the *favelas,* the expansion of social security benefits, and the creation of a universal health care system. These are long-term projects and I constantly have to remind myself that it may take years to achieve these goals.

That's why for me, working in Congress is more difficult than the organizing work we did in the *favela,* because in Congress we usually don't see immediate benefits from our work. In the *favela* everyone was working for the same objectives — the betterment of the community. It's different here in Congress. Everyone has different objectives, and the work often seems far removed from the lives of real people.

In Congress we're fighting an uphill battle against policies that place the interests of the international market above the public good. These policies continue to make the rich richer and the poor poorer. My commitment is with the poor, but the conservatives in Congress don't have the same commitment. That's why many powerful people are uncomfortable with me being a political leader. That came across loud and clear during my campaign for mayor of Rio in 1992.

If I hadn't fallen in love with Pitanga and not had his support, my campaign for mayor would have been even more difficult. It was a grueling campaign; I often worked 18 hours a day. I would go to so many different places during one day and I had to keep changing clothes. Sometimes I would go to a church in the morning, then to a *favela,* and then to a fancy reception. One time, I got so mixed up that I ended up wearing two different color shoes. I ended up having to keep a whole wardrobe inside the car.

Don't remind me of the cars we had to use! They were so old that they always broke down, got flat tires—all kinds of problems. There I'd be in my fancy outfits pushing an old car in the middle of the road. The only campaign where I had a decent car was when I ran for Senate.

You can't imagine what I have to go through in these campaigns. I don't drink alcohol or coffee, so when people offer me something to drink and I refuse, they immediately offer me some food and I have to accept. So I end up eating all kinds of things— *feijoada,* barbecued pork, sausages. They're all things I love, but they're not very good when you're on the run. Sometimes I'd get a stomachache and have to go to the bathroom really badly, but I'd be followed by a pack of reporters. You can't get any privacy when you're in the middle of a campaign.

The campaign for mayor was not just exhausting physically, but emotionally because it was very cruel. It was a very American-style campaign, with the attention revolving around irrelevant issues like who you slept with, if you smoked marijuana, those kinds of things.

My opponent had the backing of the business elite and ran a very expensive campaign. Even so, I was still ahead in the polls and had tremendous popular support. In the end, however, I lost the elections by three percent, after a series of accusations about my family were widely publicized by the media.

An enormous amount of attention was focused on a mistake that my son committed, a mistake I had no prior knowledge about. It turns out that Leleco, like 300 other public employees, had altered his school records in order to get a raise. He didn't present a false document to get the job—he already had the job. But since the salary level was pegged to the employee's education level, he and his colleagues faked their degrees to get higher salaries. The opposition, with help from the press, made this into a huge scandal. It was manipulated in such a way that it seemed as if it were not my son but me who had done this. It was terrible.

Even if I had known what he had done, do you think a mother can control her grown son? I don't interfere in the lives of my children. I tried to teach them what I could, to give them good values, but they're bound to make their own mistakes. And given the hardships they went through as children, I'm lucky they're not criminals.

What my son did was wrong and foolish, and when he realized how much it affected me and my campaign, he was crushed. I know that if he had any idea of the consequences of his action, he would never have done it. He was so ashamed of himself that I couldn't bear to even mention it to him. I remember when the story first came out in the press he looked at me as if to say, "For the love of God, don't say anything." And I never said a word. He already knew that he had made a mistake, he knew that this mistake jeopardized my entire campaign.

My poor son . . . I cry every time I think about it. When Leleco was seven he was already delivering bread at dawn, sometimes in the pouring rain. If he didn't, we'd go hungry. Every time he delivered bread he got five little rolls. We always worked hard. For years I worked as a janitor in a school where they treated me badly but I didn't say anything, because as long as I worked there Leleco got a scholarship and it was a good school. But since the time he almost died from meningitis, Leleco had difficulty learning. He went to school every day and he studied hard, but he did poorly and never finished. So how should I look at what my son did, knowing what a hard life he had?

Besides, I did similar things myself. Sometimes I altered my school documents because my grades were too low. When I was a minor, I altered my work ID to make myself older so I could get a job. The majority of blacks and poor people have altered documents. We don't even register our children on the day they're born but on the day we have the money to do it, so even our birthdays have been altered.

I'm not saying that Leleco didn't make a mistake. He did. But I've made mistakes, we all make mistakes. And we all deserve a second chance. There is no way I would reject my son because of what he did. He was born from my belly and even if he was a murderer, a robber, I'd be in prison visiting him. Besides, he's been punished many times over—his pay was docked, he paid fines and was publicly humiliated. But to this day journalists continue to harp on the issue—an issue that had nothing to do with my political platform or my campaign.

When I had to live through the attacks against my son, I suffered terribly; I was feeling weak and vulnerable, and I needed a shoulder to lean on. Pitanga gave me lots of warmth and affection, as did my sister Celeide and a lot of my friends. The regional president of the Workers Party, Jorge Bittar, also gave me a lot of support. He was with me all the time and helped me understand that this was all a political maneuver on the part of my opponent. Four sisters from the church—Ely, Luiz, Jovem and Elvira—were incredible allies who never left my side. They would always say to me, "We're praying for you, we won't let them hurt you."

One of the things that most bothers me about being a politician is when the attacks get personal. I have no problem when people challenge my political ideas, but I do have problems with attacks that are aimed at simply defaming my character. When politics gets so debased, it can't be called a democratic process. Naively, I always thought it could be different, but maybe that's why I get so hurt.

After so many attacks, I'm beginning to get thick skin and to learn how to protect myself. In 1996, when there were two major attempts to discredit me, I was better prepared to respond. The first incident, *o escândalo da banheira* — the bathtub scandal—was unbelievable. The administration was doing repairs in many of the senators' apartments. In the bathrooms, they installed bathtubs with whirlpools—which, by the way, I don't even use. When it got out to the press that Benedita da Silva had a whirlpool in her bathroom, there were full-page articles about how I was wasting government funds. I never asked for the whirlpool, and I was certainly not the only senator who had one. So why did the press pick on me?

This time I quickly realized that it was a political maneuver designed to discredit me and my party. The story came out the same day as the convention of the Workers Party that was going to pick the candidate for the mayor of Rio. So our opponents decided to blast me to pieces, in case I was planning to run.

When I learned about the scandal, I immediately issued a statement denouncing the attack. But the story kept appearing in the newspapers and TV stations for days, and I realized that the more I defended myself, the more material they had to keep the story alive. I was giving legitimacy to their absurd accusations by responding to them. So I decided not to make any more comments about it, and the scandal died.

The second incident was based on a very offensive statement made by José Pio Guerra, a leader of the government-run Small Business Association. Criticizing the way Congress was distorting a piece of legislation, he said that the bill entered Congress "looking like Marilyn Monroe and left looking like Madonna. Oh no, Madonna is too good a comparison. It ended up looking more like Benedita da Silva." I didn't take it as just a personal insult, but as an attack against all black women. I decided to go on the offensive and I got a number of organizations like the National Council for Human Rights, the National Council for Women's Rights, and Afro-Brazilian organizations to demand a public apology. I also received a lot of support from other congresswomen. I don't care if people think I'm pretty or ugly. But to compare something good in Congress with Marilyn Monroe and something bad with

Benedita, that's just too racist. I couldn't accept that.

In Brazil, public opinion is manipulated all the time, especially during election time. And it's not just manipulation of opinion we have to contend with, but outright fraud that can reach scandalous proportions. In some places the ballot boxes are ready to be counted even before the voting starts, or the boxes disappear after the count is taken. That's why I don't believe that I really lost the mayor's election in 1992. The margin was only three percent, but the PT didn't insist on a recount and I didn't make an issue of it because I didn't want to seem like a sore loser. Aside from the slim margin, I was also distrustful because we discovered that there were people involved in the buying and selling of votes who worked on the election tribunal. But there's no use crying over spilt milk.

I observed the elections in South Africa, after Nelson Mandela had been released from jail and they were holding their first democratic elections. I was amazed by the level of citizen participation and awareness, and this is in a country where there is a higher level of illiteracy than here in Brazil. They had photos of the candidates on the ballots to help those who couldn't read. The voting lasted for three days: the first day was for pregnant women and people with physical problems, the other two for the rest of the population. I was so impressed at how a country that has never known democracy managed to hold their elections in such a fair and orderly way.

It's important for the PT to observe examples like this. Remember, the PT only started in 1982, it's barely an adolescent. We still have a lot to learn.

One of the things we have to learn is how to make strategic alliances with other parties so we attract more voters. Before, the party didn't put much effort into making alliances. We used to launch our own candidates first, and then start discussions about alliances. But that's not the way to do it. We have to have those discussions before picking our candidates; if not, it's not a real alliance.

The Brazilian left is facing a great battle because the parties of the right are making alliances with the neoliberal parties. So we have to work with other parties on the left, we have to support joint candidates so we can have a greater chance of being elected in congressional, state, and municipal races.

We also have to bring a broader segment of the population into the party itself, including those in the middle class. In the beginning our theme was, *"trabalhador que bate cartão, não vota em patrão"* —workers who punch a timecard don't vote for the boss. And now we realize that workers are not only people who wear overalls. They're also people who work in the informal market, they're professors, doctors, lawyers, judges, and small and medium business people. These people have a lot to contribute to the party as well.

There was a time when the PT didn't try to negotiate with business people. We soon realized that if we didn't work out agreements, we would always be standing on the sidelines complaining but not making changes. Some representatives of the working class still criticize me when I go to speak to the business sector. They don't understand that I'm looking out for the workers' interests by trying to negotiate. This is not incoherent or inconsistent, it's just a question of tactics.

Sometimes the differences within our party make political work very difficult. It's bad enough that I get so much grief from my opponents outside the party. It's even worse when it comes from within my own party, like when the PT was deciding who would be the candidate for mayor of Rio in 1996. There was a lot of jockeying among the potential candidates, a lot of power plays going on. Despite the fact that I was leading in the polls, I didn't want to participate in the primaries because I thought that even if I won, the other candidates wouldn't support my campaign. So I decided that I would only run if there was consensus about my candidacy, and that didn't happen. The primaries are supposed to be a vehicle for uniting the party around a certain candidate, but all too often they create internal division. During the primaries, the attacks can become so heated that it's difficult to repair the damage. The winning candidate goes into the race with a fragile base of support. We have to learn how to create some parameters for the primaries so they don't end up damaging our internal unity.

Despite our limitations, it's amazing how the PT has managed to have such an impact on the political process in such a short time. In 1984 we helped organize huge demonstrations to pressure the government to hold direct elections for president, instead of having the president appointed by the two major parties. In this campaign, called *"Diretas Já"* — Direct Elections Now, the Brazilian people took to the streets in massive numbers for the first time since the 1964 coup. This movement was so forceful that it led to direct presidential elections in 1989. And the PT, with Lula as our candidate, made a spectacular showing in the elections and came very close to winning. Imagine, we almost had a metalworker as president!

Again, in 1992, the PT played a historic role when PT representatives forced Congress to investigate charges of corruption against then President Fernando Collor de Mello, and called for his impeachment. These charges led to a public outcry that culminated in Collor's resignation.

Our representatives in Congress have proposed innovative projects in education, health care and agrarian reform. Right now a coalition of conservative parties has the majority of votes and can usually veto our projects. But at least the PT plays the critical role of stretching the limits of the debate and airing controversial issues before the public.

On the local level, we have won a number of mayoral elections, and the cities we govern have become more open to popular participation. We are winning more and more local elections because the voters understand this. We also control two state governments. Our administrations keep their books open to make sure the public can scrutinize the budget and help set priorities. This open-book policy ought to be the norm everywhere, but it isn't.

Some of our city governments have received awards from UNICEF because they managed to do away with illiteracy or make major improvements in health. Even the ex-mayor of São Paulo, Luiza Erundina, despite fierce opposition during the entire time she was in office, managed to improve government services, particularly in the area of health.

But we face our difficulties when we win as well. The administration we follow usually leaves us with enormous debts that must be paid off. We must confront ongoing, pitched battles from our political opponents. Also, when you run an open administration, you promote an increased level of awareness among the population, which often results in more people getting organized and fighting for their rights. Workers have gone on strike during our administrations the same way they do when other parties are in power. Just because we're the Workers Party doesn't mean we don't have to contend with those kinds of problems.

Sometimes our efforts are misrepresented or ignored by the press. We need to find better ways to get our message out, not only to inform the public about our policies but also to give people opportunities to express their opinions and critique our work.

Problems notwithstanding, the right in Brazil has realized that the PT is a major force to contend with and is here to stay. The left now understands that the PT's aim is not to divide the progressive forces, but to unite them. And internationally, the PT has won considerable respect and is seen as a model to be closely watched.

For me personally, it's been a rewarding but difficult path. Sometimes the tension builds and builds, and I get upset. My work is very stressful, very demanding. I'm running around all the time from one appointment to another. And some people don't understand how much work it takes to be a good politician. I recently returned from Germany where I was helping to launch a beautiful project to fight hunger in Latin America. When I arrived home after an exhausting 22-hour trip, a person passed by me and said, "Look at her, always traveling instead of working!"

There are moments when I get very depressed, and I think, "Why don't I do something completely different, like go back to school to study history or political science, or spend time abroad to learn foreign languages?" As much as I try to brace myself, the media attacks get to me. When I'm under intense pressure or I'm being harshly criticized, I cry my heart out. I also get depressed when I realize that I've hurt other people by being too severe in my criticisms of them.

Politics also takes away so much from my family time. I wish I had more time to spend with my grandchildren, taking them for walks or out to the movies, eating hot dogs and popcorn. Etiene, Leleco's daughter, is 10 years old, and Nilcea has three children—Ana Benedita, who is 12, Benilton, who is 10, and Diego, who is 6. I love spending time with my family and they miss me a lot when I'm in Brasília. That's why they don't want me to run for office again. I never thought it would be so important for me to have time to stay at home, to cook, to do laundry. I like to invite the whole family over for Sunday dinner, and cook for them myself. They love my cooking, especially my *feijoada*—nobody makes it like I do.

I need to have my private moments when I can be anonymous, because in public I have to behave in such a formal way. Sometimes I'd like to have more freedom, to let out a belly laugh that only my daughter and I know how to do. The other day, I was thinking that I don't laugh as hard as I used to. I used to speak louder, too, and I've had to learn to speak more softly. I have to watch my behavior because I know that there are always plenty of people just waiting to criticize me.

I miss being treated like an ordinary person. I think it's great when people just come up very casually to chat with me. They ask, "Is it OK if I call you Bené?" And we talk like friends.

The other day, I was walking down from the *favela* with Nilcea and a woman said to me, "Where's your chauffeur? You shouldn't be going on foot!" Why not? I'm a normal person just like anyone else. Many politicians isolate themselves and lose touch with reality. When I go out shopping, people say to me, "What are you doing here?" The other day I was at a supermarket and I met my nephew, who was working there. Later his coworkers asked him in wonder if the person he was talking to was really Benedita da Silva.

Some people think I should have the kind of lifestyle other senators have and criticize me when they see me shopping or walking along the street. Others think that I live a very luxurious life for a person who comes from the *favela* and is a member of the Workers Party. No matter what I do, I can't win. I feel that people have such different expectations of me, and sometimes that makes me want to retreat inward and protect my privacy.

Pitanga's different—he's more open in public. Wherever we are, he kisses me and shouts out loud, "I love you, Benedita." I think that's fabulous, and I ask myself how he has the courage to do things like that. I wish I could be more spontaneous, because I feel inhibited by my public image. But Pitanga knows how to get to me. He gives me one of his delicious smiles and says, *"Sacode o esqueleto, Bené!"* —Loosen up, Bené. And little by little, I start to give in.

Like that song *Maria, Maria* by Milton Nascimento and Fernando Brant, I'm a woman who needs to *"amar como outra qualquer no planeta"* —to love like any other woman on this planet. When I'm in Brasília the phone bill is huge. I talk to Pitanga every night—it's our ritual. And if he's out late and doesn't get a chance to call, we make sure to talk the next morning. It's our way of trying to reconcile our personal and political lives.

I have no illusions that my presence here in the Senate is going to change the minds of the people who have power or that it's going to change the world. I never thought this would be easy. I was never one to think that if you studied hard you could make it, or if you worked hard you'd get rich. And I know that in this political work, the victories are few and far between. Our society is so divided between rich and poor, black and white. But the fact that I'm a black woman from a poor background allows me to break a lot of stereotypes. I want to give people hope. I want to seize the opportunities whenever I can, grab them *com unhas e dentes* — with my nails and teeth, and take them as far as I can.

Chapter Four
From Life After Death
to Life After Birth

*Bene, age 16, at the wedding to her first husband
Nilton Aldano da Silva*

Nunca fui uma negra que se calasse.
Eu protestava. Protestava contra tudo.
Protestava tanto que acabei protestante.

I was never a woman who kept quiet. I always protested. I protested against everything. I protested so much that I ended up becoming a Protestant.

—Benedita da Silva

My mother practiced the Umbanda religion. Umbanda is a traditional Brazilian religion, what some would call a syncretic mixture of Catholic and African elements. But my mother, like other *umbandistas,* didn't like their religion to be called syncretic because that implied it was not legitimate.

After my mother moved to Rio de Janeiro, she held Umbanda ceremonies in our house in Chapéu Mangueira. Although the house was made out of scrap wood, it was always neat and clean. And when there was a ceremony going on, the house would be decorated with altars, candles, and special foods for the *orishas.* My mother would sit in the middle of the room on a tall wicker chair, looking like an African queen.

My mother helped many people. They would come to her when they were very unhappy. She would perform the ceremonies, and they would leave smiling. I remember rich people who came with problems that we didn't have. They were unhappy because they were fighting over money, inheritance, those kinds of things. Sometimes even politicians and other powerful people would show up incognito. They didn't want anyone to recognize them or see them there. That's because for centuries, practitioners of Umbanda, like other Afro-Brazilian religions, were persecuted by both governments and other religious groups.

Ever since the time of slavery, Afro-Brazilian religions were seen as a form of resistance against the elites. They also represented a threat to the conservative Catholic Church, which was always very strong in Brazil. When I was a child, the police would come to the *favelas* to break up the ceremonies. My mother used to say that she never got caught because the *orisha* gods protected her and stopped the police from finding out where the sound of the drums was coming from.

When I was young, I used to help my mother perform the ceremonies. She raised me to believe in Umbanda and hoped that I would follow in her footsteps. I didn't, because I ended up choosing another religion. But later in life I realized that my mother's spirituality greatly influenced my political work. I saw my mother helping people all the time, because in addition to being a priestess she was a midwife. She made food for the mothers and gave clothes to the newborns. My father would yell at her for giving away the little we had, but she'd say, "José, remember when we lived in Minas and we didn't even have food to eat? Now that we have a little yard to grow our own food, we should share what we have with those who have less." The entire neighborhood knew and loved my mother.

The ceremonies in our house would go on and on, sometimes until four in the morning. The first part of the ceremony was preaching and the second part was dancing, singing, and drumming. I used to help my sister sell pastries during the break in the middle. If I'd sell the whole tray she'd let me eat two pastries. I was supposed to sell each pastry for 50 cents, but instead I'd sell them for 60 cents and pocket the extra money until I had enough to buy one for myself.

I never became a strong believer in Umbanda. That's because like any other religion, Umbanda has its dogmas. Every *orisha* god has its rules and as a young girl, I would go crazy when my mother wouldn't allow me to do things because it went against the rules. I didn't like to help her out in the ceremonies, especially during Carnival week, because it meant I couldn't go out in the street and dance. I also had to attend lots of ceremonies at the end of the year.

On December 31, everyone in Rio goes to the beach to see the ceremonies and wait for the new year. I would drive my mother crazy because after midnight, when the religious ceremonies were over and we were supposed to go home, I'd run off to join the people dancing samba through the streets. I'd be all dressed in white from the ceremony, so everyone knew that I was an Umbandista. I always felt ashamed because people were so prejudiced against Umbanda at the time.

I was also very rebellious, not only against the religion but against a lot of the rules we had in the house. For example, we were not allowed to speak during mealtime, and I could never understand why. At that time, it was my job to feed the pigs we had in the backyard. I would always try to play with the pigs and talk to them, but they were only interested in eating and wouldn't even look up at me. One evening, when we were eating dinner, I decided to break the silence. So I stood up and said, "I'm not a pig that eats with my head down." Everybody laughed and that was the end of the silent meals.

But it wasn't so easy to change my parents when it came to religion. If I came late to the ceremonies or did something disrespectful, I'd be punished. Sometimes my parents would hit me with their hand, sometimes with a stick of bamboo. When my mother got sick and couldn't run after me, I would walk towards her, so she could hit me. I knew it would help her release her stress and feel better.

After my mother died, my older brothers Roserval and Tonho continued to perform the Umbanda ceremonies. I worked with them until I was 18 years old. But by then, I was very involved in community work, teaching in the *favela* and working in the neighborhood association, and all the people I worked with were members of the progressive wing of the Catholic Church. We worked in small groups called *comunidades eclesiásticas de base,* Christian base communities, where people would come together to talk about the problems they faced in their everyday lives and how they could take action to solve them. These groups were part of the church movement based on liberation theology, which preached that the church should work with the poor to better their lives. After working with them for a few years, I decided to join the Catholic Church.

Liberation theology is very different from the mainstream Catholic Church, which cooperated for many centuries with the system that repressed blacks, indigenous people, and women. The church hierarchy worked hand in glove with the state, especially during the military dictatorship, when it was complicit with the government's gross violation of human rights.

The mainstream Catholic Church encourages the poor to be submissive by promising them happiness in heaven. Liberation theology, on the other hand, defends the right of men and women to seek happiness here on earth. It defends the right to have a piece of land to grow food and the right to a livable wage. Liberation theology is about raising people's consciousness and fighting against oppression.

This progressive wing of the church has been persecuted even within the Catholic Church itself. Some of its leaders, like Leonardo Boff, a person I greatly admire for his courageous work in challenging the status quo, have been expelled from the Church.

With its emphasis on empowerment of the poor and social justice, liberation theology fits well with my principles as a Christian and as a politician. I continue to work with the Christian base communities because they've made a great contribution to community organizing in Brazil.

My work in the Christian base communities was critical for my political development. But it was also frustrating because we were suffering a great deal of repression during the military dictatorship, and the repression made me feel impotent and powerless. The military seemed so entrenched in its power that it was difficult for me to see the light at the end of the tunnel.

I was also going through an extremely difficult period in my personal life. I was feeling overwhelmed by poverty and hunger. I had lost two children and had a terrible abortion that left me with physical and emotional scars. And my husband Mansinho was in bad shape, since his problems with alcohol had gotten worse. Poor man—he suffered a lot and so did I. Many people, including my daughter, told me that I should leave him. But I felt responsible for him. He was the man I loved, he was the father of my children, he had grown up in the streets and had managed to overcome his past and build a family. But he never managed to get steady work and this crushed him. He tried and tried—I know he did. He turned to alcohol as an escape, as a way to numb the pain.

I started to feel so desperate during this time of my life that I even contemplated suicide. I was in great need of emotional and spiritual support. That's why, when I was 26, I joined a branch of the Evangelical Protestant Church called *Assembléia de Deus*, the Assembly of God. It gave me a new kind of inner peace and tranquillity that I needed to help me reflect on my life. It provided me with a way to cope with things that were out of my control. After all, that's what faith is all about.

People can find this faith in any religion. Some find it in Umbanda or other Afro-Brazilian religions such as Candomblé; others find it in the Catholic or Protestant Church. In my case, it was the Evangelical Church that fulfilled my deep spiritual need. But the Evangelical Church did not fulfill my political and social needs, my desire to work with the community. It wasn't involved in these kinds of activities, so despite my conversion, I continued my social work with the Christian base communities.

Many people have a hard time understanding how someone with my political views would become an Evangelical. It's true that the Evangelical church has a very conservative wing and that progressives like myself are in the minority. In Brazil, many Evangelicals have a reputation of intolerance toward other religions, especially the Afro-Brazilian ones. Throughout Latin America, Evangelicals have often aligned themselves with conservative and even repressive governments; others have discouraged people from getting involved in politics. They focus on the individual instead of the community, and are only concerned about life after death. I say fine, it's okay to contemplate life after death, but let's not forget about life after birth.

There are other rules in the Evangelical Church that I've had no problem accepting. For example, Evangelicals are not allowed to drink or smoke, which is fine with me. I never liked to drink so that was no hardship. As far as smoking, when I was young I smoked over two packs a day, so it was good that I was motivated to stop.

Something that was harder for me was the prohibition on dancing. I loved to dance when I was young, and I was a great dancer. When I was 23, I was elected Miss Samba of Copacabana during the celebration of the 400th anniversary of the founding of Rio de Janeiro. But I stopped dancing when I became an Evangelical because it's frowned upon by the church.

Some people in my church condemn all types of dancing, even Carnival, and look down on people who dance. I think it's fine for us to choose not to dance, but I don't think it's right to condemn others. In my mind, this dogmatic kind of thinking was introduced into the Evangelical Church as an excuse to discriminate against certain cultural traditions, particularly Afro-Brazilian traditions. As for me, I have no problem with other people dancing, and I appreciate dance as a very significant component of Brazilian culture.

I've changed some of my habits to conform with my religion, but despite the strong influence of conservatives in the Evangelical Church, I've always maintained my political independence. I'm also careful not to use the church as a vehicle for my political work. If some brothers and sisters in the church support my political initiatives, it's because they personally identify with my beliefs and think of me as a good leader. But I would never exploit their faith to gain political support, and I would never hide my true political beliefs to gain the support of the more conservative members.

The conservative Evangelicals don't represent all Evangelicals, and certainly don't represent all Protestants. I consider the Protestant Church to be a revolutionary one because it was born out of a break with the Catholic Church. There are progressive Protestant churches all over the world. You see this very clearly in the United States, where the struggle for civil rights was embraced principally by black church leaders like Reverend Martin Luther King and Reverend Jesse Jackson. In the United States, the majority of blacks are Baptist and this church is involved in the struggle against social inequality. Another good case is South Africa, where people like Bishop Desmond Tutu were on the forefront of the anti-apartheid movement.

I remained in the Assembly of God Church for almost 20 years and it gave me the spiritual force I needed. But, unfortunately, I had to separate from that church when I got married to my second husband, Bola, because they don't allow their followers to marry someone outside the religion.

When Bola and I decided to get married, it was really important for me to get married in a church. So I contacted Pastor Caio Fábio, who represents the progressive wing of the Pentecostal Church. I liked him and his church, and he said he'd be happy to marry us. Bola and I got married there and that's the church I belong to today. For me, marrying a person with different religious beliefs didn't imply a change in my spiritual life. In fact, loving and being loved gave me more strength to face life's ups and downs and to explore my spirituality.

No matter what church I belong to, I get my strength and religious conviction from the Bible. The Old Testament speaks of a God who fought for the oppressed and against slavery. It speaks of a God who values human beings and condemns all attempts to turn them into objects of exploitation and domination. Political issues I defend, like agrarian reform, have religious significance to me. God created the earth, and he never gave land titles to anyone. Turning the land into private property goes against the biblical concept that we all have the right to share God's bounty.

The Bible also teaches us that women should be respected. Jesus defended prostitutes against that hypocritical society where they were stoned to death. Could it be that the prostitutes had sex by themselves? Wasn't it the supposedly upright family men—the ones who were most judgmental and the very ones who created the laws condemning prostitutes—who would seek them out on the sly? I think that laws can only be enforced if they are respected by the people who wrote them. Laws should exist to democratize relations and guarantee citizens their rights. They shouldn't be used as an instrument of repression.

Some people think that I shouldn't quote the Bible because it doesn't have a scientific basis. But the Bible talks about the history of civilization, and through a critical reading of the Bible, I learned that the structures of inequality have been repeated over and over throughout history. I didn't need to read Marx to understand inequality. The Bible talks about laws that repress people, about corruption, about the large landowners stealing the land from the poor.

In the Senate, I deal with people who represent the interests of the big landowners. I deal with landowners who say they're Christians, but when poor peasants occupy their land to grow food for their families, they uses violence against them. I try to understand why these men think they need so much land. I remember a story from the Bible that talks about a man who accumulated a lot of land, filled his silos with food and said, "Now I can fill my soul." And God answered, "You crazy fool. Tonight I will come for your soul and all your possessions will do you no good." And it's true. Accumulating possessions will not make you a better person or feed your soul. We're all going to die one day, so instead of hoarding, why not spend your life helping people live with dignity in a world where we all have food and a roof over our heads?

When I speak in Congress about the need for agrarian reform, I don't use leftist language to get my points across. I say things like, "Forget about communism and socialism. Let's talk about helping our brethren. Let's look at agrarian reform as a Biblical mandate." Some senators from other parties find it curious to hear a representative of the Workers Party talking like that. They laugh and say, "Oh, look at the new party line the PT has. How do you like that!"

But all these ideas *are* in the Bible. The Bible is full of revolutionary ideas and that's why I don't feel any contradiction between my faith and my politics. Some narrow-minded members of my church criticize me for being in the Workers Party, and some narrow-minded members of the party criticize me for being an Evangelical. But in my view, God doesn't have a political party, so we can belong to any party we choose. For me, faith and politics are perfectly compatible. The stronger my faith, the more strength I have to engage in politics. As a member of the Pentecostal Church and a member of the PT, I tell people that I'm a "PTcostal."

Since its founding, the Workers Party has always had close ties with religious groups, particularly the progressive wing of the Catholic Church. Rigid Marxists within the party frown upon these ties, as if religious people had infiltrated the party and tried to set its agenda. But it's not like that at all. At the same that the PT was being formed, progressive members of the Catholic Church were creating Christian base communities and getting involved in projects to help the poor. The PT and the progressive Catholic Church had a lot in common. And the ties that these religious people had with the poor in the *favelas* and the countryside were critical in strengthening the grassroots base of the PT. You also have to realize that these religious leaders supporting the PT were not acting on behalf of the Church, because the Church is not supposed to be involved in politics and the hierarchy of the church never supported our party. They were simply acting as individual religious people who identified with the PT's platform in favor of the poor.

Orthodox Marxists in the party don't understand that the PT needs to be open and embrace different sectors of society, including the religious community. I don't consider myself a Marxist, but I do consider myself a revolutionary. Jesus was more revolutionary than any leftist party I've ever seen. He always spoke out against oppression.

While there are members of the PT who criticize the church, particularly the Evangelical Church, there are Evangelicals who are deathly afraid of the PT and have launched strong attacks against it. Some of them don't like the PT because they think of it as the party of the Catholic Church, others see the PT as a bunch of "communists who eat babies." But this is changing as Evangelicals learn more about the PT.

An historic opening between Evangelicals and progressive politicians took place at a forum we held in 1991 called "The First National Forum for Discussion and Understanding between Evangelicals and Progressive Parties." Just a few years earlier it would have been inconceivable to initiate a dialogue between Evangelicals and Marxists, so this was a rare opportunity for the two sides to meet.

More than 300 people participated, including pastors, religious and political leaders. For two days, we discussed and reflected on issues of common interest to both Christians and politicians committed to social justice. We discussed the growing influence of conservative Protestant churches in Latin America, and how we could channel that influence into more progressive outlets. We shared our concerns about how the poor were being oppressed for the sake of the "free market." In contrast to a society that deifies profits and material goods, we reaffirmed our commitment to a society that protects human rights and guarantees its citizens jobs, health care, and education.

It was a momentous gathering because both sides realized that we could join forces to advance our common ideals. At the end of the conference the Progressive Evangelical Movement wrote an open letter to the Evangelicals. We expressed our grave concern about the apathy of the majority of Evangelicals toward the serious social and economic crises facing Brazil. We recognized the need to expand the vision of our faith and promote a more profound understanding of the Bible. Most importantly, we called on Evangelical leaders and followers to work with neighborhood associations, popular councils, unions, and other grassroots organizations in their efforts to measurably improve the lives of the poor.

While many Evangelicals participated with the PT in Lula's campaign for president in 1989, these ties became even stronger after the Forum. When I ran for mayor of Rio in 1992, I had a lot of support from the Evangelical community. Many Evangelicals now see PT candidates as upholding the biblical ideals of justice, peace, love, and freedom. They realize that while we may not be saints, we are certainly not the devil! Today there's even an Evangelical committee within the PT, and there are many Evangelicals within the party—just as there are many Protestants, Catholics, believers in Afro-Brazilian religions and atheists.

Of course, many religious supporters of the PT disagree with the party's stand on certain issues. One of the most controversial issues is abortion, which, except in the case of rape, is illegal in Brazil. Women with economic means can get around the illegality and can find doctors in expensive clinics who will help them. Poor women end up having dangerous, clandestine abortions, which have led to thousands of deaths.

I'm personally against abortion because I think it's bad for a woman's physical and spiritual well-being. But I believe in the right of women to have abortions if they so desire. I definitely defend abortion in cases of rape, because the Bible says that sexual relations should take place with love, not with violence. And while abortion in the case of rape is legal, women often have to go through such a long, bureaucratic process that they end up having the babies because too much time has passed.

Despite my personal objections to abortion, I think that it should not only be legal, but state supported. Because if abortion were legalized but the government did not provide abortion facilities in public hospitals, poor women would not benefit from the legalization. They would be forced to continue using knitting needles and to suffer serious health consequences.

Another controversial issue between religious believers and the PT is homosexuality. This issue divided the PT during the creation of the party's platform for the national elections of 1994. Religious PT members like myself struggled with the church's position, which condemns homosexuality. After many months of discussion, the PT decided to include the demands of the gay and lesbian groups in its platform.

I supported that position. I think the question of sexual orientation is a very individual thing, a personal option. Personally, a homosexual relationship would not be appealing to me. What I like in a relationship is to discover the "other," someone who is different from me, and to learn from that "other."

But I don't accept discrimination against homosexuals, and it's true that homosexuals face a lot of discrimination in Brazil. They are discriminated against in the workplace, and can rarely be open about their sexuality without facing intimidation. They are also sexually exploited in places like prisons and suffer from great violence if they end up prostituting themselves on the streets. The worst of all are the barbaric killings of homosexuals that have taken place in Brazil over the years.

I believe that same-sex couples should have the right to things like inheritance, social security and pensions. Why not? Why deny these rights to gay couples who loved and cared for each other throughout life?

Perhaps the reason that I have a more open attitude toward these issues than most people in my church is because my family had all kinds of people in it, including prostitutes and homosexuals. One of my cousins was a homosexual. He was really mistreated at home — his brothers would beat him up all the time — so he came to live with me. Later on in life he decided to become an Evangelical and he stopped being a homosexual because the church did not accept it. But I always tried not to interfere in his personal life and to respect his options.

Another controversial issue like homosexuality is the issue of divorce. Despite the teachings of both the Catholic and Protestant churches, I've never been opposed to divorce. I think marriage should last as long as there is love and understanding, and I don't understand why the church thinks it's necessary to guarantee a life-long social contract. When the person performing the marriage ceremony instructs the couple to say that they will be united "until death do us part," I ask, "What kind of death? Physical death, or the death of their love?" When love dies, why should the couple continue together? If people aren't happy in their marriage, they should have the right to build a new relationship.

I have no problems defending divorce, but I recognize that there are class differences when it comes to divorce. The legalization of divorce in Brazil helped women in the upper social classes, women who could get things like alimony and child support. But it didn't help poor women. When poor women get separated, they don't go to court and fight for financial support from their husbands because there's no money to fight over. Poor women know that it's up to them to take care of their children on their own.

Take my daughter Nilcea. She's still not legally divorced because her former husband never appeared to sign the divorce papers. She can't ask him for financial support because he doesn't have any money or assets. But at least Nilcea is lucky in that she has a new partner who respects her and is like a father to her children. I don't have any problem with the fact that they're not formally married.

It's hard for me to understand why some people in the church have such a rigid view of women's rights and sexuality. I suppose it's related to the fact that women still don't have much power within the church. In the Evangelical Church, many people continue to think that women should keep quiet and submit themselves unconditionally to the will of men. These ideas serve to reinforce prejudices that already exist in society.

But today many Evangelical women have gone beyond the phase of merely complaining, a phase that left us immobilized. As religious women, we have started to demand—and achieve—changes in individual and social relations within the church. We don't want to be seen as just "assistants" to the men in church activities. We consider ourselves partners with God and with men. That's why we must fight against all forms of gender-based domination and must work together with men to transform our society.

I get inspired when I read in the Bible about some of the fabulous women who stood up for their rights or defended the poor. We need more Christian women with the courage and daring of Sifra and Pua, midwives who, under the Pharaoh of Egypt, risked their lives by saving male babies who were condemned to die. They broke the ethics and codes of the Pharaoh's laws to do God's work.

We need more Christian women with the courage of the daughters of Zelofeade, who risked their lives when they fought for the right to inherit their father's land, at a time when women did not have such rights. The actions of the daughters was so radical that Moses was perplexed and had to consult with God about it. God told him that their demands were legitimate and amazingly, their demands became law and were included in the Old Testament.

We need more Christian women with the strength and sensitivity of Deborah. She was a judge who eschewed the luxury and privileges of her position. She held court beneath a palm tree where she listened to the suffering and pain of the poor.

Where are our Sifras and Puas to defend the rights of street children today? Where are our Deborahs to advocate in favor of the landless, the illiterate, the homeless, the hungry? Where are the daughters of Zelofeade to fight for women's rights?

We live in a country of cruel inequalities, where the luxury and privilege of a small minority are sustained by the misery of the majority. This unjust social structure has its roots in laws and institutions that promote inequalities and make victims out of millions of people who don't have the basics to live a dignified life. So we can't be neutral or remain silent. We Christians—men and women—can't isolate ourselves from social injustices and take comfort in false speeches that try to hide those injustices. We must listen to our God, a God who cures the sick, feeds the hungry, frees the oppressed, takes care of the children, and unmasks the hypocrites. This is a God who tells us to break with the institutions that promote injustice.

Hunger, poverty, and exploitation of the oppressed people in the Third World have forced theologians to rethink their ideas about faith and the mission of the church. Every theology can choose to defend life; it can choose to take concrete positions and actions in the world in which we live. This socially active type of church rejects the use of religion as the "opiate of the masses." Instead, it acts as a catalyst in the search for social justice and equality. Instead of focusing on the afterlife, it puts forth the powerful notion that we can enjoy "eternal life" in the here and now. It is this kind of sensitive, engaged and loving church that has captured my heart.

Chapter Five
Feminism With Passion

"What an amazing experience to be at the Women's Conference in China with tens of thousands of women from all over the world!"

I love when Gal Costa sings that song "Teco, Teco" by Pereira da Costa and Milton Villela:

Não fazia roupa de boneca nem
tão pouco comidinha com as garotas do
meu bairro, que era o natural.
Subia em poste, soltava papagaio, até
meus quatorze anos era esse o meu mal.

I didn't make clothes for my doll or play house with the girls in my neighborhood, like I was supposed to. I'd climb lampposts, fly kites. Until I was 14, this is what was wrong with me.

B ack in sixteenth-century Brazil, the Jesuit priest Antônio Vieira preached that a woman should only leave her home three times in her life—when she was baptized, married, and buried. Since then, Brazilian women have certainly gotten out of the house. We've struggled for the right to education, and today 60 percent of university graduates are women. We've struggled for the right to work, and today almost half of the workforce are women. We've struggled for the right to vote, and today we are even running for office and winning elections.

Women in Brazil have come a long way, but not far enough. We're still relegated to less prestigious professions—teachers, secretaries, clerical and domestic workers—and we earn half the pay that men do. We may be winning elections, but only six percent of the congressional representatives are women.

While few men today dare to openly defend the idea that women are inferior, sexism still permeates our society. In the media, women are portrayed as sexual objects and their bodies are used to sell all kinds of products. Sometimes sexist attitudes appear in more subtle ways—disguised in our schoolbooks or in the words of popular songs. The message is that girls should be well behaved, cute, and sweet, and boys should be smart, sharp, and competitive.

Gender roles are not natural or determined by biological differences. They're socially constructed roles, and vary according to the culture and the time period. Intuitively, I have always questioned these stereotypes since the time I was a child. I liked to build my own toys and do the same things boys did. I played marbles. I climbed trees to pick fruit. I was one of the few girls who worked in the market.

But many women are influenced by the stereotypes promoted by the media. They obsess about their weight—going on crash diets, then gaining the weight back and dieting again. I don't worry about my weight. I'm not going to kill myself because someone thinks I should be skinny. Plus, who says that fat people are ugly? I also don't kill myself doing exercises that are too hard on my body. For me, taking care of my body means taking a shower. I love taking hot showers; that's my kind of exercise.

I'm not interested in looking like everyone else. I refuse to buy certain clothes just because they're in style. I'm also not the type of woman who worries about wrinkles and is afraid of getting old. I'm proud of being a grandmother. I enjoy my age, I don't try to hide anything.

Men also suffer from stereotypes of what a "real man" is supposed to be, especially when it comes to sexuality. Women often buy into these stereotypes about men, and create their erotic fantasies. I know we can't be totally rational when it comes to sex, but through my work as a nurse's aide, I learned that *tamanho não é documento*—size isn't everything. When it comes to sex, there are more important things.

These gender stereotypes make it difficult for women to be assertive. Men are more accustomed to being in control and they don't want to take orders from women. I see this in my own professional life. Sometimes I have difficulty with men I work with. They belittle my political position and call me *mulher mandona*—a bossy woman. I've even overheard men calling me *negrinha metida a besta*—an arrogant nigger. That's because I don't like to follow orders. I can't stand someone telling me how to act or what to do.

Breaking out of traditional gender roles has always been a challenge in my personal relationships. My second husband Bola was wonderful, but sometimes he found it hard to adapt to a wife who was truly his equal. He would admit that he was sexist and he'd say, "Give me time, Bené, I'm trying to change." We had some difficult moments because I felt a kind of competition, particularly when it came to our political careers. We tried to keep our own political spaces, but many people saw me as Bola's wife. When I was running for Congress in 1986, we had a fight because after he had agreed to coordinate my campaign, he decided to become a candidate himself for deputy governor of Rio. I thought it was a bad decision because it would jeopardize my campaign. And he felt like I wanted him to renounce his own career for mine. So I ended up agreeing that we should both run.

It was difficult for Bola to accept that he wasn't the traditional head of the family. I'm sure he felt like a married man, but I don't think he ever really felt like his house was his home. That's because when we got married he came to live in my house, which was awkward for him, and also because my salary was higher than his was. If I went out to buy something for the house, he'd say, "You should have told me and I would have paid half." But because I earned more money, I didn't think it was fair to ask him to share all the expenses. While I tried hard to make him feel comfortable, he never got used to it. His first wife, Baleca, was a wonderful woman who took care of him. Our relationship was different. I was devoted to our marriage, but I didn't have time to be a traditional housewife. Some nights we'd come back from work at the same time and he'd sit down and pick up the newspaper or turn on the television, waiting for me to cook dinner. But I was used to sharing the household tasks with my first husband Mansinho. So we both had a lot of adapting to do.

Now, in my relationship with Pitanga, it's easier for me to keep my independence and individuality. In 1993, right after our honeymoon, he moved in with me in Chapéu Mangueira. He was easy to live with because he was used to taking care of a household. When Pitanga and his wife separated, his two children Rocco and Camila stayed with him and he raised them on his own. Every man should have the experience of bringing up children, particularly daughters. It's the best cure for breaking down gender stereotypes.

Pitanga is very good to me and my children. When I'm angry, he let's me yell and scream and just listens. Then he says, "Don't get so worked up, Bené. Let's talk about this calmly." Sometimes he complains about me being too independent. When I leave the house early in the morning while he's still asleep, he says, "Why didn't you wake me up? You took a cab? That's ridiculous, I could have driven you. You know I like to spend time with you."

Sure, I'm independent, but I do like to do special things for Pitanga when I get the time. Pitanga likes it when I cook and serve him his food. He jokes around with me and says, "You fought so hard to be liberated and then you end up serving me." But I don't feel oppressed when I cook for him. I enjoy it and wish I had time to do it more often. Sometimes Pitanga drives me around to my appointments—not because he has to but because he wants to. Doing things for each other is simply part of building and maintaining a good relationship.

Many times women in positions of power feel they have to act like men to gain respect. We have an expression to describe someone who is assertive. We say they *"põe o pau na mesa,"* which literally means they "put their dick on the table." I consider myself a feminist, but I don't want to have to act like a man to gain respect. I believe I can be assertive and a true feminist without losing my femininity.

I also don't think that feminist women have to be stiff and hide their emotions. Strong women are women who know how to laugh and cry, women who love with passion, women who nurture. I'm an extremely warm and caring lover. I have a very strong personality but in the privacy of my own home, I express all my feelings, including those considered by some to be a sign of weakness.

I know how to flirt and use my charm. I like to dress well and I know that men admire well-dressed women. I admire men who look sharp, too. Sometimes when I see an attractive man, I think of the romantic song *Girl from Ipanema* that goes, *Olha que coisa mais linda, mais cheia de graça*—Look at that beautiful thing, how full of charm. . . . I certainly appreciate a handsome man, a muscular body. But that doesn't mean that I would ever use a man as a sexual object, like men do to women. The most important thing in a relationship is to feel an intellectual affinity. When that happens, that first impression based solely on physical attraction becomes secondary.

And just because I look at other men doesn't mean I'm unfaithful to Pitanga. I'm faithful to him because I respect and trust him. For me, fidelity has to be a mutual agreement. I can't stand this double standard where people think it's acceptable for men to cheat on their partners, but if women do it's a big scandal. If it's adultery when a woman sleeps with another man, then it's adultery when a man sleeps with another woman.

In Brazil, the concept of "conjugal fidelity" is actually written into the Civil Code. It's supposed to work both ways, but in reality it only applies to women and so it becomes an instrument to preserve male domination. That's why I'm trying to change the wording of the Civil Code, eliminating any reference to "conjugal fidelity" and replacing it with "mutual respect and consideration." The latter is a more advanced concept and reflects women's struggle for juridical equality. It also reflects my own feelings that the most important element for a good partnership is not fidelity but mutual respect.

You wouldn't believe the controversy that my suggested revision provoked. Some men in Congress were scandalized and said, "If you're going to get rid of fidelity, you might just as well get rid of marriage." They accused me of advocating free love and attacking marriage as an institution. But I really believe that fidelity in marriage should come from reciprocal love, not from the imposition of punitive laws or obsolete rules that are only applied to women.

I have a very liberated attitude when it comes to sex. I always talked to my children about everything. When they wanted to know how babies were born, my husband didn't know what to tell them, so I explained everything. I gave them all kinds of information about sex. One time my son came home with gonorrhea and my husband was horrified. I was the one who had to take care of him, and I had no problem with that. I also don't have a hang up about my body or nudity. Even today, I take off my clothes in front of my children.

I never put pressure on my daughter to be a virgin when she married, even though that kind of pressure was very common when I was growing up. Most parents were really uptight. They were constantly fretting over whether their daughters *"pularam a cerca"*—jumped the fence. If the girls got caught with their boyfriends, the parents would create a big scandal and sometimes even throw their daughters out of the house. My parents had this type of mentality and my sisters suffered because of it. One of my sisters became a prostitute and had to leave the house. I felt sorry for her and we continued to have a good relationship.

Although I've always tried to pass these liberal values on to my children, my daughter Nilcea is more conservative than I am. My granddaughter Ana Benedita, however, takes after me. Nilcea says, "This child is going to give us a headache." And I say, "Of course she is, *ela vai botar pra quebrar* — she's going to drive us crazy." She's already very assertive and I'm sure she's going to be a very independent woman. But I want her to go out in the world with her eyes open to the difficulties that women face.

One of the real difficulties that many women confront is sexual harassment. Sure, it's nice to feel desired by a man. A sexual advance, if it's done respectfully, makes you feel good and is simply part of the game between the sexes. I'm not offended if a man admires me sexually, but I won't accept an aggressive come-on. I know how to throw a bucket of cold water on a guy's advances when I have to, but not all women are able to protect themselves. Many times women have to perform sexual favors in order to get a job. And to get ahead professionally, they have to put up with come-ons and lewd behavior from their bosses.

Sexual harassment not only exists in the workplace, but any place where men and women get together. When men first look at women, they're usually undressing them with their eyes. Men feel powerful through sex, especially if they have sex with a lot of different women.

Many men want to have their *"mulher de casa"*—woman at home—and *"mulher da rua"*—woman on the street. The prostitute is seen as someone with whom they can be more sexually intimate and get greater sexual pleasure. Their wives are expected to be more modest. Taboos and dogmas don't allow the wives to fully explore their sexuality. This pushes the men to play out their sexual fantasies with prostitutes, whom they feel they can exploit in whatever ways they please.

Black women bear the brunt of this exploitation, particularly when it come to white men. There is this impression that black women are *"mais quentes"*—hotter, so men feel free to exploit them more. Black women are considered more pleasing sexually, but these men usually don't want to make a commitment to them. Black women are considered good enough for screwing, but not good enough to marry.

These sexist attitudes lead to one of the most serious problems in Brazil today, which is violence against women. When I was a federal deputy, I helped organize a special Congressional commission to investigate this issue and we were shocked by our findings. We discovered that over 300 cases of violence against women were reported every day. In fact, we discovered that Brazil was the world champion in terms of violence against women!

A large part of the violent crimes against women are committed by their husbands and lovers. Seventy percent of the violence against Brazilian women takes place in the home. We found case after case of girls impregnated by their own fathers and stepfathers, and women who are beaten by their husbands every day.

I myself had horrible fights with my first husband, Mansinho. If he was drunk and we had an argument, he'd lose control and hit me. I'd defend myself and hit him back. It was terrible. One time we had such a bad fight that I fainted. My father, who lived with us, panicked because he thought I was dead. He tried to kill Mansinho. My children started crying and screamed, "Help my mother. Don't kill my father."

You might wonder why I just didn't leave him. I had been brought up to believe that marriage was for life. And I did like him and he was a good father to our children. These awful fights started after he'd lost his job and was going through a crisis. One time he hit Leleco and bruised him badly. When I came home I found Leleco rolled up in a ball in the corner, crying. I realized just how sick Mansinho was, because I knew he really adored his son. Another time he hit Nilcea. She ran out of the house in the middle of the night with one shoe on and one shoe off, and came to the hospital where I was working. I told my supervisor what happened and asked if I could leave. She was reluctant but she let me go home. When I got home, I had a long conversation with Mansinho. I told him he couldn't hit his daughter like that. He felt badly and came to the bus stop with me so I wouldn't be alone so late at night. I think I never left him because I felt sorry for him — he was really a sick man.

This problem of domestic violence became a priority for the women's movement in Brazil. To deal with this issue, women successfully fought for the establishment of women's police stations, *delegacias da mulher*, run by and for women. There are now 182 of these stations, located in several states. They take care of the physical and psychological needs of women who have been raped. Regular police stations don't offer this kind of help — abused women usually feel intimidated and humiliated when they go to a regular police station after they've been raped, or after other forms of domestic violence.

The number of reported cases of sexual abuse has risen greatly since these women's police stations were started. Women who had remained silent for years decided to denounce their aggressors, even if it meant running the risk of further marital conflict. Due to the success of these police stations, I made a proposal to expand them throughout the country. But unfortunately, it's up to the individual states to allocate the money, and many state governors are not committed to this project.

While these police stations are helpful in that they provide women with a place where they can file complaints against their abusers, they don't prevent women from being abused. Men may be intimidated by the fact that they have to testify in court, but the court system works in their favor. Just look at the record for men who kill their wives—80 percent of them are found not guilty because they committed the crime "in defense of their honor."

At the same time I was investigating violence against women, I was also participating in a Congressional committee on another violation of women's rights: mass sterilization. We were astonished to discover how many Brazilian women were being sterilized. We found that unlike other countries, where a range of birth control methods are used and sterilization is rather uncommon, in Brazil sterilization is the number one method of birth control. Of the 70 percent of women between 15 and 45 who used some kind of birth control, 44 percent were sterilized. In the developed countries, the average is 5 percent.

The rate was highest among poor, black, and indigenous women. In some states, like the impoverished northeast province of Maranhão, the rate was an astounding 80 percent! The high incidence of sterilization among black women has been denounced by the black movement as a racist policy.

Sometimes girls as young as 13 are sterilized. I was sterilized when I was 22 because I felt at the time that I had no other choice. I regretted it later when I wanted to have another child. If it wasn't for being poor, I would have had more children, since for me, children are a blessing. In my case, I knew that I was being sterilized. But many women don't even know what's happening to them or don't quite understand that it's irreversible.

The mass sterilization of Brazilian women is something new. Before the 1970s, only 5 percent of Brazilian women were sterilized. After that, foreign governments and organizations invested large sums of money to control Brazil's population growth. The World Bank alone gave Brazil over 600 million dollars to set up family planning institutions in seven of the poorest states in the country. Instead of providing women with different family planning options, the main method of birth control promoted by these institutions was sterilization.

Some people say that I'm paranoid when I say that the First World is imposing these population programs on the Third World. But I really believe that the rich countries are determined to reduce the population of the poor countries, even if these countries aren't overpopulated. Look at the case of Brazil. It's larger than the continental United States, but our population of 160 million is much smaller than the 250 million in the United States.

First we were told that we had to reduce our population to pull ourselves out of poverty. But sterilization doesn't guarantee that a woman will find a job, a school for her kids, or a decent house to live in.

Next we were told that we had to reduce our population because we were destroying the environment by depleting the earth's resources. But the world's environmental crisis has more to do with the consumerism of the developed countries than too many people in poor countries. The richest 20 percent of the world's population produces about 75 percent of the world's pollution. Here in Brazil, it's not the poor who are destroying the environment. It's the big timber and mining companies, and the large cattle ranchers.

I'm not saying that we don't want to plan our families. We do. In the cities, many poor women prefer to have small families, and they need information on the best methods available. In the countryside, it's different. People often want to have lots of children because children start working by the time they're seven and contribute to the family income. These people should not be forced to have fewer children because some foreign agency wants them to. There's a big difference between family planning and population control.

We need to provide women with different birth control options, and we also need to educate men. Women should not have the sole responsibility for family planning, and we have to encourage men to consider options like vasectomies, which are less risky than sterilization for women.

A high rate of population growth has to be seen as a symptom of a larger problem, which is poverty. It's been proven the world over that population growth goes down as people—especially women—become better educated and their standard of living goes up. While the rich countries want to get rid of the poor, we in the poor countries want to get rid of poverty.

These issues of mass sterilization, violence against women, and gender inequalities became the focus of my work during my first term in Congress. The years I worked intensively on these problems, from 1986 to 1988, were the best moments of my life. We were just coming out of the dictatorship and we were in the process of writing a new constitution. Women's groups around the country were mobilizing, and we worked like mad to make sure that our rights were included in the new constitution.

Since Brazil's independence in September 7, 1822, we've had seven constitutions and none of them included women's rights. In fact, there were parts of the old constitutions that were patently sexist. Women who weren't faithful to their husbands didn't have the right of inheritance. Women didn't have the right to bring charges against their husbands, even if their husbands beat them.

Today, Brazil's Constitution is among the most progressive in the world in terms of women's rights. It declares discrimination against women illegal, and says women must receive equal pay for equal work. It guarantees 120 days of maternity leave for women and eight days of paternity leave for men. It says the state has the responsibility to guarantee that people receive information and access to non-coercive family planning.

We worked hard to get language in the Constitution that guarantees the rights of domestic workers—an issue that is very dear to me. The Constitution spells out that domestic workers should have the same rights as other workers—including the right to earn the legally specified minimum wage, and the right to paid vacations and paid holidays.

I also fought to guarantee the rights of women prisoners. Women in prison now have the right to keep their children with them during the months the children are breast-feeding. And we won the right for women prisoners to have conjugal visits, which were previously only granted to men.

But it's one thing to have good laws on the books, and another to implement them. Right now, many of the rights guaranteed in the Constitution are constantly violated. Brazilian society must internalize these rights and demand that they be upheld.

Look at the continued discrimination against women in the work force. Although it's illegal, women are still fired for getting pregnant. Many companies ask for a pregnancy test before hiring a woman, and won't hire her if the test is positive. It's still hard for women to get promoted to managerial positions, and when they do, they get paid less than men.

Brazil's three million domestic workers are still terribly exploited. They receive miserable wages and are forced to work long hours.

When they work as live-in maids, they often live in truly slave-like conditions. If they are young girls who want to study, it's usually impossible for them to combine their work with school. Employers continue to treat maids as second-class human beings.

And we shouldn't forget that on top of discrimination at work, women go home to face the double shift of household chores and taking care of the children. The poorest and most overworked women are those in single-parent households: in Brazil, one in five households is headed by a woman.

At the political level, there is still very little space for women in Congress. When we organize investigations into "women's issues" such as violence against women or mass sterilization, they are given short shrift. The major decision-making power remains concentrated in the hands of a small group of men. As I've said time and time again, power is still male, white, and rich.

That accounts for the fact that every time we take two steps forward, we're forced to take one step back. Right now we're faced with the risk of another backlash from the new conservative wave that is permeating Brazilian society. They're talking about restricting the small gains we've made, such as the right to abortion in the case of rape, which is presently the only situation in which abortion is permitted.

Whether in the home, the workplace or the halls of Congress, women still have little power. We worked so hard to get a Constitution that's strong on women's rights, but for the majority of poor women, the constitutional rights we won are pretty meaningless. Poor women are still faced with the daily dilemma of how to survive and feed their children. The girls born and raised in the *favelas* still face few career options apart from crime or prostitution.

In the beginning, the women's movement, which started out as a middle class movement, had a hard time relating to poor women. They didn't understand that the issues most important to poor women in the *favelas* were how to get running water, how to get our husbands out of the bars, how to get a job. Issues about our bodies and sexuality weren't priorities, like they were for wealthier women. The right to abortion—which has always been a key issue for middle class women—was secondary for us. It's true that poor women were dying from botched abortions, but our day-to-day poverty was so grinding that coping with our daily needs came first.

The gap between poor and middle class women became really clear to me in 1968. That year, my house was destroyed by a storm and we were left homeless. Desperate, I asked for help from some of the women in the feminist movement who worked with us in the *favelas*. I was shocked when they said they couldn't help me. They were interested in talking to us about women's rights, but their idea of sisterhood didn't include helping a sister in need. It made me realize that we women in the *favelas* needed our own space to discuss *our* problems, like how to get a roof over our heads and shoes for our children. We started to get together to talk and help each other in everything from taking care of our children to doing each other's nails and hair. We concentrated on our day-to-day problems, but eventually we started to talk about everything from social issues to our bodies and our sexuality.

Today, the women's movement is much broader and there is greater understanding and solidarity across classes. Now there are women's groups all over Brazil focusing on all kinds of issues—women's health, reproductive rights, domestic violence, affirmative action. These issues not only cross class lines, but international boundaries. They are problems that affect women in every part of the world. That's why we need to work together on an international level to find creative ways to guarantee women's rights. This became clear to me when I had the great opportunity to attend the Fourth International Women's Conference in China in 1995.

It was an amazing experience to be with tens of thousands of women from all over the world! It's shameful how little media coverage there was of the conference in Brazil, given the historic nature of the meeting and the fact that Brazil sent the largest governmental and non-governmental delegation of any country.

There were plenty of controversial issues at the conference, especially issues related to sexual and reproductive rights. Sometimes we stayed up until 2 or 3 in the morning debating. In these discussions, there were two camps—those who wanted to expand women's rights, and those who wanted to respect traditional customs and preserve the status quo.

The Brazilian delegation fit squarely in the first camp—it was extremely progressive in its positions and had a great impact on the debates. We tended to have the same positions as women from Europe, the United States, and Canada. The more conservative women were Muslim women from countries like Iraq, Morocco, and Sudan, as well as Catholic delegates from the Vatican and its allies like Argentina and Guatemala. They often looked at issues from a purely religious context, instead of a world context in which there are a lot of different ethnic groups, cultures, religions, and even people with no religious beliefs at all.

The progressive delegations wanted to have women's rights considered universal, fundamental human rights that should be guaranteed by governments everywhere. The conservatives wanted to qualify those rights, taking into account cultural and religious differences. The Muslims, for example, don't believe that women should have the right to inheritance because it goes against their religion. The liberals wanted to press governments to guarantee that adolescents have access to sex education. The conservatives wanted to leave it up to the parents to decide how and when their children should receive this information.

Another source of tension was between women from rich and poor countries. Delegates from rich countries wanted to focus on sexual rights instead of the most pressing issue confronting women, which is poverty. We pointed out that it was insensitive for the rich countries to focus on sexual freedom when so many women still live in misery and have no economic independence.

For all the women at the conference, one thing was clear: in spite of the gains made throughout the world, no country treats women the same way men are treated. In no society do women enjoy the same opportunities as men. Seventy percent of poor people in the world are women, and over two-thirds of the world's illiterate are women. Women still earn less than men, and they continue to be the last hired and the first fired. The world over, women still have less access to political and economic decision-making.

Even the nations that define themselves as advanced democracies have not eliminated sex discrimination. Looking at the world from a woman's perspective, no country in the world is democratic.

That's why whoever we are, wherever we live, we women can't let down our guard. We must keep on fighting to gain new ground. And at the same time we organize women, we can't forget our responsibility to educate men. Because the fight for women's rights is not a war between the sexes, but a struggle to create a true partnership with men. I'm convinced that the more rights we gain as women, the freer men will be. Equality between the sexes is the key to a better world for all of us.

I feel full of hope when I look at my granddaughter and remember the day she was born. On March 8, 1985, International Women's Day, I was speaking at a women's rally. Somehow, as I spoke, I had a premonition that my daughter Nilceia was going to give birth to a baby girl. I told the crowd: "Another Benedita is coming into the world. I know that she and many others will keep our struggle alive!" After that, Nilcea didn't have a choice but to name her daughter after me. Her name is Ana Benedita. She, as well as my other grandchildren, is a great inspiration in my life.

Chapter Six
Exploding the Myth of Racial Harmony

*Benedita, on a visit to the United States, met with
Reverend Jesse Jackson*

Miscigenação, que maravilha
garantiu a presença de todas as etnias
reservou para cada
uma função
Nas matas vivas, verdes cabocla
vivem os povos da floresta
nas favelas a negrada
nas penitenciárias abarrotadas
nas ruas famintos pedintes
Miscigenação, que maravilha
me esmero
me curto
me quero
gerente de banco,
general,
governador,
presidente, prefeito, senador.
Veja que beleza
não há racismo, não há
Universidade aberta para toda gente
capa de revista
manchete de primeira página
sucesso no jornal nacional
me vejo toda na televisão.
Imaginem se nessa terra há
    discriminação!

Miscegenation, how marvelous
it guaranteed the presence of all
    ethnicities
it reserved a special role
for each one.
In the living green jungle
live the *cabocla*, the people of the
    forest
The blacks in the *favelas*
in the overcrowded jails
in the streets hungry beggars.
Miscegenation, how marvelous
I primp
I delight myself
I love myself
bank manager,
general,
governor,
president, mayor, senator.
Look how great
there's no racism, none at all.
Open university for everyone
magazine cover
front page headline
sensation in the national news
I see myself on TV.
How can you say there's
    discrimination here!

—Benedita da Silva

A foreign visitor coming to Brazil for the first time might ask herself: Where are all the black people?

Starting with the plane, it would be difficult for our visitor to find black passengers or even crew members. In the airport she'll see few blacks, perhaps some porters and taxi drivers. Arriving at the hotel, she'll have a hard time finding blacks eating in the restaurant or relaxing by the pool.

If she starts flipping through a magazine in her room, she won't see any black models in the ads. If she switches on the television, she probably won't see a single black performer. It's even more unlikely that she'll see blacks in the commercials.

But as soon as she steps outside and starts to walk around, she's certain to see more blacks. Her first encounter will probably be with black street children, who will ask her for spare change, or for the leftovers on her plate.

So how can people say that Brazil is the world's largest racial democracy? Many white people insist there's no racism here. You'll hear them say, "I have a black friend who comes over the house all the time." But in the homes of whites, blacks are usually present only as servants or gardeners.

The truth is that racial democracy in Brazil only exists in school books and official speeches. The elites in Brazil have promoted this myth of racial harmony to make people accept certain forms of discrimination and to deny the need for affirmative action.

Of course, if we compare racism in Brazil to racism in the United

States or South Africa, we'll find major differences. These countries forced blacks into separate ghettos, they created segregated schools for black children, they made blacks ride on separate busses or in the back of the bus, and so on. In Brazil, none of these mechanisms of segregation were imposed by law. But if we compare the color of the residents in the *favela* Mangueira with the color of the residents in well-to-do Ipanema, or the color of the passengers in the crowded trains from the poor suburbs with the color of the passengers on the downtown subway, we find virtually the same segregation.

Many Brazilians argue that this separation reflects class differences, not racism. Even some people on the left think that we shouldn't focus on the issue of race because the major issue is one of class. They say that if we built a society with a fair distribution of wealth, the position of blacks would automatically improve. But I disagree. Blacks suffer because they are poor, but they are poor *because* they are black.

I remember one time when I was participating in a debate on race. All the other panelists were white, middle class women who insisted that there was no racism in Brazil. The debate became very heated and emotional. At one point, one of the women accused me of promoting reverse racism because I said we needed affirmative action for blacks. While this woman was going on and on, I started writing a poem. When she finished talking, I read the poem out loud. I said:

Nasci mulher negra	I was born a black woman
me fizeram homen e branco	They turned me into a white man
me castraram, me impediram	They castrated me, they wouldn't
de ir	let me go
mas não vou compactuar-me	But I'm not going to
com isso	accept this
vou gritar, soltar minha voz e	I'm going to shout, let my voice
me fazer livre	cry out and make myself free
para continuar a ser, mulher	So I can continue to be a black
negra.	woman.

I was born black and female, but this racist society so excluded me that at one point in my life I really wanted to be a white man. When I was a child, I would go to the homes of the rich to deliver my mother's laundry, and people would say, "You can't come in this door, you have to go around to the back door." I was always taught that my place was with the poor, the blacks, the marginalized. It made it very hard for me to appreciate my own self-worth.

Throughout my youth, I felt the color of my skin was the color of evil. I remember once I wanted to be an angel in the school procession, and the teachers said I couldn't be an angel because there were no black angels. Black represented everything dark, ugly, and sinful, while light represented everything pretty and virtuous. That's the way things were portrayed to me.

According to the media, beautiful women were light-skinned. I could never hope to fit this standard. When I was in school the other kids would call me *nega maluca* —an ugly nigger. I was big and black and had "hard hair." I longed to have straight hair. I felt so ugly and rejected. I'd try to hide my hair under a scarf.

When I was in elementary school, I was a very dedicated student. I had very neat handwriting and I took such good care of my notebooks. I would take pieces of newspaper and cover the notebooks carefully so they would be tidy and pretty. I'd sit up front and pay close attention to the teacher. One day, at the end of the year, the teacher told me that I had received the best grade in the class. I went home all excited and invited my mother to go to our graduation party. She was so proud and on the day of the party, we got all dressed up and went to school. When we got there, the teacher said that there had been a mistake and that I wasn't the best student after all. From then on, I felt rejected and discriminated against. I went from sitting in the first row, to the second, third, and fourth, and finally I ended up sitting way in the back. My handwriting got smaller and smaller, and it became so small that the teacher could hardly read it.

I hated being a black girl and dreamed of being something that I wasn't. One day, I was so distraught that I took a tub that my mother used to wash clothes, filled it with bleach and water, and took a bath in it to see if I could make my skin lighter.

People who reject their blackness are like the *jabuticaba*, which is a native Brazilian fruit that is black on the outside and white on the inside. Racism is so internalized that many blacks refuse to call themselves black. That's why there are literally dozens and dozens of terms for describing someone with dark skin—*mulato, feijãozinho, criolo, pardo, café com leite, marrom, bombom.*

This mentality affects the way people respond to surveys on race and makes it hard to get an accurate picture of just how large the black population in Brazil really is. The government census says that blacks make up 44 percent of the population, but many black groups and academics dispute this and say the figure is much higher. A UNESCO study says blacks make up 70 percent of the population, which is probably closer to the truth.

There are other reasons why the definition of race is so complex in Brazil. In the United States, anyone who has black blood is considered black, even if they have light skin and light hair. But in Brazil, a person's race is not determined solely by their origin. A person with black ancestry who has light skin may be considered white, particularly if he has a good job, lives in a middle or upper-class neighborhood and is well-educated.

For example, my stepdaughter Camila Pitanga is certainly black in terms of her roots—both her father and mother are black. But she's light-skinned, middle class and has a good job, so people don't consider her black. But if a person with the same physical characteristics was poor and illiterate, lived in the *favela,* danced samba and was a believer in Umbanda, she would be considered black. So people are "lighter" or "darker" depending on their economic and social status.

It's ironic that despite the pervasive discrimination against blacks, all Brazilians identify with black culture. Daily life in Brazil is infused with *"africanidade"*—African-ness. The African influence is the seasoning that gives special life, color, and flavor to our national soul.

We see this not only in religion and in Carnival, but in the shape of our bodies and the gestures we make. These characteristics are so strong that white Brazilian women are totally different from white European women. African culture has an influence on the way white Brazilians look and act, too; it influences their entire physical being.

Whites in Brazil—both men and women—have adopted many aspects of black culture. They eat African-based dishes, enjoy black music and find comfort in black religion. But it's curious how black culture maintains its black identity no matter how many whites participate. The Portela samba school, for example, is said to have more whites than blacks, but Carnival is still considered part of black culture. There are many Umbanda groups whose members are mainly white, but Umbanda remains a black religion.

It's impossible to understand the complexity of race in Brazil today without looking back at the historical and social roots of race relations. People aren't racist because they're evil; they're racist because they've inherited a legacy of racism that comes from centuries of slavery.

I'll never forget the moment when I visited Gorée Island in Senegal. It was in 1992, when I was invited to an international meeting organized by the Gorée Memorial Foundation. Gorée is the island where slaves from all over Africa were gathered and separated according to their age, beauty, strength, and health, before being put on slave ships headed for the Americas.

I felt such anguish when the guides told me how families were torn apart—men from women, children from their parents. I thought of my own ancestors. I saw the tiny cells where the slaves were crowded together like animals. Imagine a big person like me, who is five feet nine inches tall, held in a cell that was only two feet high and filled with 20 other slaves! And can you believe that on top of the prison was a restaurant, a bar and a clubroom? So white people would be sitting around having a grand, old time while in the cells down below black women and men were trembling with pain, hunger, shame, and fear.

The Portuguese colonized Brazil and then used black and indigenous slaves to build their fortunes. For more than three centuries blacks produced the wealth of this country, working on the sugarcane, coffee, and cotton plantations, and in the gold, diamond, and silver mines.

Black women worked in the plantations and in the master's house as maids and wet nurses. Many were sexually abused by their masters and their lives were marred by violence. When they got pregnant, they often aborted because they didn't want to bring their children into slavery.

By the nineteenth century, there were about three million black slaves. In fact, Brazil was the country that received the greatest number of slaves—some 35 percent of all the slaves in the New World landed in Brazil. Today, we have the second largest black population in the world, surpassed only by Nigeria.

The white elite was deathly afraid of a slave uprising. They feared that blacks in Brazil would follow the example of the uprisings in Haiti or Cuba, where blacks were influenced by the revolutionary ideals of the French Revolution—the principles of liberty, equality, and fraternity. That's why for years after the abolition of slavery, the Brazilian Constitution contained a clause that explicitly prohibited black immigration.

Brazil was the last nation in the West to abolish slavery. The first step was in 1871, with the declaration of the *Lei do Ventre Livre,* the Law of the Free Womb. This determined that all children born after that time would be free. Since the children were free, but their parents were not, these "free" children were separated from their families, thrown out on the streets and forced to fend for themselves. The street children of today are the legacy of this law.

In 1888, Princess Isabel signed the law that finally abolished slavery. But contrary to what official textbooks say, that process did not occur peacefully. Our schoolbooks glorify the white colonists and explorers, but say little about Brazil's long history of slave revolts and the creation of *quilombos,* or townships made up of runaway slaves. Palmares in northeast Brazil, the best-known *quilombo,* was a multiracial society where runaway slaves, as well as poor Indians and whites, lived together in harmony. They built a thriving community with their own agriculture and through trade with neighboring villages. They had a strict moral code and their own justice system.

The Portuguese Crown was intent on destroying Palmares, since its reputation was spreading throughout the country and inspiring other slaves to organize. The colonizers sent 17 military expeditions to Palmares, but all of them failed. The people resisted heroically for almost a century. The Portuguese also tried repeatedly to co-opt their leader Zumbi, offering him land, freedom, and other benefits if he would dismantle the *quilombo.* But Zumbi was incorruptible.

It was only in 1696, with the use of cannons, that the mercenaries sent by the Portuguese finally managed to destroy Palmares. Zumbi was captured and executed. As a warning to others, his head was placed in the center of Recife until it decomposed. But Zumbi's stature only grew in the eyes of the people, and he became a legend. Zumbi is today considered a hero of the black movement.

Today we also recognize the role of black women in resisting slavery. Black women played a major role in the slave rebellions and in building the *quilombos.* In the eighteenth century, for example, Rainha Tereza was the queen of the *quilombo* Quariterê for two decades. Born in Angola and forced into slavery in Brazil, she led a group of Indians and blacks to run away and start a *quilombo* near the border of Bolivia. During her rule, she organized a well-developed defense and agricultural system. The Portuguese destroyed the *quilombo* in 1770, murdering and imprisoning its inhabitants. Tereza was captured, and she killed herself by taking poison.

Even after the abolition of slavery, blacks continued to live in miserable conditions. The majority had no access to education. The few who were lucky enough to get a piece of land had no resources to work the land. The landless were unable to find decent jobs because they couldn't compete with the more educated workers coming from Europe. Many families fell apart, and women often became the sole support of the family, usually working as domestic servants.

This disadvantaged position continues today. Blacks get less education, earn less, eat more poorly, and die earlier than whites. Life expectancy for blacks is eight years shorter than for whites. Illiteracy for blacks is 37 percent compared to 15 percent for whites. Even during the days of apartheid in South Africa, there were more blacks in South African universities than in Brazilian ones.

Blacks are virtually absent from senior government. There is one Cabinet minister of mixed descent, and none of the country's 23 state governors are black. Of the 559 members of Congress, only 7 consider themselves black. In the Armed Forces, you'll find few or no blacks among the generals, admirals, and colonels. In the business world, 82 percent of businessmen and high-level administrators are white.

While blacks make up the poorest sector of the population, black women are at the bottom of the ladder. Ninety percent of black women have only completed elementary school and their presence in the university is negligible. While black women have always been in the workforce, we are seen as ignorant and only capable of the most menial jobs. Our role is to clean the houses of white people and take care of their children.

Few people recognize how the labor of black women has contributed to the emancipation of white women. When white women began to integrate themselves into the workforce, it was black women—working as maids, cooks, and nannies—who made this possible.

Despite the fact that black women entered the workforce long before white women, they earn 48 percent less than white women in the same professions. Only two percent of black women have professional jobs; the majority are employed in agricultural labor or services. Eighty percent of domestic workers are black.

Even as nannies, we're discriminated against. It wasn't long ago that people would put ads in the papers saying: "Looking for a white nanny." The black movement fought to make this type of language illegal. Now the ads say "good appearance necessary," which is a euphemism for light skin.

When blacks do manage to move up the social and economic ladder, they still can't escape racism. Successful blacks are considered arrogant and uppity. That's why blacks still don't feel comfortable in roles traditionally occupied by whites. The idea persists that blacks should know their place—that they should stick to the *favelas* and the poorest paying jobs.

There are exceptions, of course, like the great soccer player Pelé. Pelé says he never felt discriminated against. But he's a millionaire and his life is totally different from the lives of the vast majority of black Brazilians. Pelé was educated and trained by the white elite. His social circle is mostly white, which is not the case for the majority of blacks. So naturally he doesn't feel the same kind of discrimination that most blacks do.

Sometimes this discrimination is totally blatant, as when blacks are abused by the police. This happened to my own son, who was arrested and beaten simply because the police mistook him for someone else. They didn't believe him when he said he was my son, because a black couldn't possibly be the son of a congressperson.

I encounter this mentality all the time. Once, Pitanga and I were driving in Brasília in a car with official license plates when the police stopped us and made us get out of the car with our hands on our heads. They were suspicious of us because we were two blacks driving around in an official car.

When people don't know who I am and see me in my car with the driver, they think that I'm a maid out doing chores for my boss. Sometimes when I open the door to my apartment in Brasília, people ask me to call the owner, Benedita da Silva. One time a government driver rang the bell and said, "Tell your boss that I'm waiting downstairs for her."

When I was first elected to Congress, I would get in the congressional elevator and the guards would stop me and say, "Sorry, this is only for congresspeople." And I'd answer, "Oh, what a coincidence. I'm a congresswoman." They would get so embarrassed and apologize. The same thing would happen with my black friends. One day, Hermogenes came to visit me in Brasília and the security guard was shocked when he saw this big, black guy with dreadlocks coming in. I think he must have been even more startled when I told him that Hermogenes was my political advisor.

The other day, I went to a store to buy my grandchild a birthday present and the security guard stopped me to check my bag. I noticed that plenty of white customers walked in and out carrying big bags, but nobody checked them. It was embarrassing because everyone was staring at me like I was a thief.

I've lost count of the times I've been stopped before entering a building and asked for identification. One time our party president Lula and I had a meeting at the office of one of our supporters. I got there early and the doorman stopped me in the lobby. It was only after the arrival of Lula, who's white, that the doorman allowed me to go up.

The racist nature of our society became really clear during my campaign for mayor of Rio. Once the elites of Rio understood that there was a real possibility that a black woman could become mayor, they panicked. They felt so threatened by the idea that their city would be run by someone who came from the ranks of the poor, black community that they cast aside the myth of racial democracy and began their racist attacks. I started to get nasty letters and threatening phone calls. White men on the street would yell at me and make obscene gestures. They'd shout things like, "Your place is in the *favela*," "Get back to the kitchen," or "Hey monkey, go back to your tree." People joked that if I was elected, I'd change the big statue of Christ that overlooks the city for a statue of King Kong.

The same kind of racism surfaced during my 1994 senate race. I received anonymous threatening phone calls and dozens of letters saying disgusting things like:"We should go back to the time of the slaves when we could whip the niggers to keep them in their place."

Some of these threats are probably coming from racist, neo-Nazi groups. There are so-called skinhead groups in São Paulo, for example, that have been threatening anti-racist human rights groups. People tell me I should be more careful because some of these guys are really crazy. They say I shouldn't walk around the streets and in the *favelas* by myself, that I should ask the government for protection. But I never wanted to have a bodyguard, and although I must admit that sometimes the attacks scare me, I refuse to be intimidated.

It's always frustrating to go to the police to report a racist incident, because they don't take it seriously. Before I was a politician, they'd say to me, "My advice is that you just forget about it. You're a poor woman, and this will never go anywhere." Now they tell me, "Oh, don't make a big deal about it. You're an important public official. You shouldn't lower yourself for such a small thing."

Sometimes the racism is subtle, but it still hurts. I remember the day I took office as a newly elected senator. All of us senators were in the Congress building, celebrating the momentous occasion with our families. A group of people passed by my office and I heard them say, "Look, this is going to be the office of Benedita da Silva.

There'll be all kinds of goings on here, they'll even be making offer-
ings to the gods and dancing samba." They all had a good laugh.

Their comments didn't just mock black culture, but mocked me
as a senator. I doubt someone would go by the office of a white
senator and say, "I bet there'll be all kinds of classical music and
opera coming out of here." If they did, they certainly wouldn't say
it in a pejorative way. Unfortunately, black culture is still considered second class.

This kind of mentality is also reflected in the press. In January
1997, the magazine *Veja* published an article accusing me of *"exibi-
cionismo descarado e oportunismo sem rodeios"*—shameless exhibition-
ism and blatant opportunism. They said that the fact that I had
appeared in the popular TV show *O Rei do Gado* —the Cattle
King—showed a lack of respect for my constituents and said that
I had appeared as a witness in the murder trial of the famous TV
star Daniela Peres only so that I could be in the spotlight. They
chided me for abusing official privileges, like using the VIP room
in the airport, spending a weekend in the beach resort Angra dos
Reis, and taking trips abroad. They also chastised me for having
translated my resumé into English, French, and Spanish.

The article was so nasty that it elicited a public outcry, like this
letter that says, "All politicians are self-promoters, some spend fortunes on this. So singling out Benedita da Silva is simply gross
racism. The article implies that because the senator is black and
comes from the *favela,* that's where she should stay. The senator, in
my opinion, is an example to poor blacks that they, too, should
have access to places usually reserved for whites. So what if she
appeared in a TV show. You consider this disrespectful to her constituents, but I haven't talked to anyone who feels that way. You also
say that she asked to be a witness at Daniela's murder trial, but any
fool knows that people don't become witnesses simply because
they want to—they must be summoned by the court. And if the
senator spent a weekend at Angra dos Reis with socialites and

artists, so what? You think she should only go there to do the socialites' laundry? And this comment about using the VIP room and porters at the airport. How absurd! Do you think she should carry her bags on her head? When other politicians travel abroad, it's considered a benefit for our country. Why isn't that true for Benedita da Silva?"

To fight against the racism that still permeates our society, we've been trying to build a strong black movement. But due to the complexities of race issues in Brazil and the reluctance of many blacks to embrace their own identity, this has been difficult. It was particularly difficult during the dictatorship, because the 1967 Law of National Security prohibited even the discussion of racism. After the dictatorship, groups promoting black culture and black rights began to crop up all over the country. Today there are hundreds of these groups. Some organizations focus primarily on cultural identity — music groups, dance ensembles, religious organizations. Others focus more on research and advocacy in order to influence policy. And there are a number of wonderful black women's groups around the country that work on a range of issues from health to political representation to education.

One of the issues the black movement successfully organized around was ensuring that the 1988 Constitution protected our rights. We managed to pass an amendment that made racial prejudice a crime without bail and with no statute of limitation. This law hasn't modified people's behavior, but at least it gives us legal support. For the first time, we have the possibility of punishing those who commit racist acts.

We also managed to get lands that were once *quilombos* turned into national historical sites. And high schools must now include a curriculum on black culture, slavery, and the history of Africa. But we have not been successful in our efforts to win recognition for the principle of affirmative action, which is something we must continue to fight for.

I've been working with the black movement to push for legislation that would require that 40 percent of the actors in both the TV shows and the commercials be black. When you watch TV in Brazil, you'd think we were a European country, full of people who look like Scandinavians. In the commercials, you see pretty white men and women eating yogurt, driving shiny new cars, opening savings accounts, and dousing themselves with perfume and deodorant. Have you ever seen a black person sipping whiskey in a TV commercial? You'd think that blacks only drink moonshine. Have you ever seen a black child in an ad for children's toys? The only time you see blacks in commercials is when there's a family planning campaign and they're trying to convince us to have less children.

In TV shows blacks are rarely the main characters. They usually appear as waiters, criminals, security guards or maids. You rarely see black doctors, lawyers, poets or philosophers. The TV executives say that blacks are not good for ratings, but the soap opera *A Próxima Vítima,* the Next Victim, portrayed a black family and was very popular. This helped us gain more support for our proposal to increase the visibility of blacks in the media. But we've encountered strong resistance from the TV networks and we still don't have enough strength in Congress to pass legislation.

The networks say that if they accept a quota for blacks, then Japanese, Italians, and every other ethnic group are going to want a quota, too. Our response is that we're not a small minority— we're more than half the population. And these other ethnic groups did not come here on slave ships. That's why I think it's totally justified to have affirmative action measures for the black community. We're now introducing affirmative action measures for women within our political parties and we must do the same with respect to blacks. These measures will give us more access to educational and job opportunities, and will better reflect the ethnic plurality of our society.

Look at the United States. Although the black population there is a minority, I think that blacks in the U.S. have struggled and achieved more. This is true not only from an economic standpoint but from an organizational standpoint as well. American blacks have been more successful than we have in gaining access to all levels of education. Proportionally, the number of illiterate blacks in the United States is much lower, and the number of blacks in the university is much higher. Blacks in the U.S. are better represented in the media and in cultural institutions. There are more politicians who represent the black community—from Jesse Jackson to the Congressional Black Caucus to mayors and local officials. And there is a black middle class—even a black elite—that has race consciousness and supports the black movement.

On the other hand, I think that the deepest wound in the United States continues to be the racial division. In the United States, even with its advanced economy and technology, the black population is extremely marginalized. This marginalization leads to racial violence, like the uprisings in Los Angeles after the incident in which the police who beat Rodney King were absolved of wrongdoing. The racial conflicts in the United States should be a warning to all of us. When marginalized people perceive their government institutions, particularly the justice system, as biased, they will rise up against them.

Take the case of Mumia Abu Jamal, a black man in the United States who is on death row, accused of killing a police officer. Many people in the United States and all over the world think that racism is at the heart of his case. There were so many inconsistencies in the trial, but the government has refused to call a new one. Mumia says that all black prisoners are prisoners of a political system based on the devaluation of black people. His case also reflects the discriminatory way in which the death penalty is applied to people of color in the United States.

Both Brazil and the United States live in constant racial conflict. It doesn't help to try to sweep these problems under the rug. Both countries are like powder kegs ready to explode and the responsibility lies with the politicians who shut their doors on the poor, refusing to help them get access to the minimum conditions of housing, work, food, and education. We must change our priorities. Instead of investing enormous sums of money building prisons, we should invest in supporting the marginalized minorities and in reactivating our economies.

Given the similarities between both countries, it's critical to build relations between blacks in the United States and Brazil. I'm very interested in understanding the achievements of the American blacks, what they have gained through affirmative action, and also understanding the current backlash against affirmative action. We must search together for forms of resistance based in our African cultural roots. We must exchange experiences that can strengthen our struggles and search for ways to unify blacks in the Americas.

White people start to feel threatened when they hear blacks talk about unity. When we question the dominant structures and demand greater participation, they accuse us of reverse racism. My opponent in the Rio mayoral race used to accuse me of polarizing society between rich and poor, white and black. But I didn't invent this polarization. Come on now. It's ridiculous to label blacks as racists because we want more opportunities in the workplace. It's ridiculous to label blacks as racists because we want to earn a livable wage, or because we want our culture respected.

I'm not trying to be divisive. On the contrary, fighting racism is a way to unify us. For this is not a problem that just affects blacks, it affects the whole society we live in. The struggle against racism is not a struggle against whites; it's a struggle to build a society where the different cultures live in harmony.

My great-grandmother Maria Rosa understood this. Every May 13, the day we celebrated the abolition of slavery, my mother would have a big reunion in our house with all the relatives. My great-grandmother would remind us how our family had been torn apart by slavery—some of her children had been sold and she never found out what happened to them. She'd tell us how important it was for the rest of us to stay together and fight for our rights. "Blacks must have pride and self-respect," she'd say. "Blacks must resist!"

She didn't say these things with a feeling of hatred against whites, but with love and warmth. How could she hate whites? Black women like my great-grandmother nursed many white babies and cared for them like their own children. No, my great-grandmother never preached hatred. Even though we were brought here on slave ships, she taught us to love this country and all its people.

Chapter Seven
Democratizing the Land

Benedita with indigenous leader Raoni

Terra,
pedacinho do meu chão
plantei couve, plantei milho,
também arroz e feijão,
vieram os homens,
veio a chuva,
a seca,
inverno, verão.
Aguardei a primavera
da esperança de colheita
mas ela não veio,
                    não.
Terra,
já é tarde
o sol declina,
breve vai anoitecer.
De manhã, bem manhãzinha
vou conversar com você
Temos muita afinidade
somos fêmeas
somos pó
somos gêmeas.

Land,
a little piece of my earth
I planted kale, I planted corn,
also rice and beans,
the men came,
the rain came,
the drought,
winter, summer.
I waited for spring
hoping for the harvest
but no, it didn't come.

Land,
it's too late
the sun is setting,
it will soon be night.
In the morning, at dawn,
I will talk to you.
We have a lot in common
we are female
we are dust
we are twins.

—Benedita da Silva

We have a song in Brazil that goes *"Todo dia era dia de índio,"* —every day was the day of the Indian. You could say that before the arrival of the Portuguese colonizers in the sixteenth century, but nowadays Indians get only one day—April 19. On that day, you'll find all sorts of commemorations, from infantile, folkloric games in kindergartens to cheap political demagoguery, like photos of the President walking down the ramp of the Presidential Palace flanked by indigenous leaders. Each year, the media seem more and more bored by these commemorations. This year the national media gave more coverage to Beatles member Paul McCartney's visit to Brazil than to the Indians.

The other 364 days of the year, the indigenous people are forgotten, or worse yet, abused.

In February 1989, I went to the Amazon for the First Meeting of Indigenous People of Xingú, where more than 300 participants gathered to condemn the construction of a hydroelectric dam. In Congress, I had been working with indigenous leaders to create legislation that would guarantee their rights in the new Constitution, so it was very moving to see my old friends—Paulo Paiacã, Raoni, Marcos Terena, Ailton Krenak. I feel very close to the indigenous struggle because we have a common history of discrimination. They received me so warmly that at the end of my speech everyone was crying. After the meeting, they performed a beautiful traditional dance celebrating the corn harvest.

I remember a very dramatic moment during the conference that highlighted the intensity of the indigenous struggle. There were TV cameras from all over the world covering the event. At one point, a young Indian woman named Tuíra Caiapó walked towards the Planning Director of the hydroelectric dam, carrying her baby in one hand and a huge knife in the other. In front of all the TV cameras and participants, she put the knife to his throat, threatening him for the damage he was inflicting on her community. Everyone was stunned. When she finished berating him and calmly stepped back, the journalists ran towards her and asked her if her threats were real. She answered, with great dignity, "I don't have to kill someone to teach him a lesson."

The Caiapó women are very powerful and exert a strong leadership role in their communities. I wish there were more women like Tuíra in Brasília!

The indigenous way of life has been threatened ever since the arrival of the Portuguese conquerors, who came to the "New World" armed with the sword and the cross. The sword was to force the Indians into subservience, and to kill those who would not obey. The cross was to drive the Western soul and faith into their hearts. The conquerors demonized the Indians' beliefs and hailed the superiority of the "Western God," a God who legitimized the enslavement of the natives in the name of faith and progress.

The Portuguese went further and further inland in search of gold. They destroyed the Indian villages, kidnapped their leaders, captured and killed their inhabitants. Those who were captured were turned into slaves. By the nineteenth century, there were about one million Indian slaves, suffering from the same cruel and inhumane treatment as blacks.

Indigenous society was torn apart and millions died fighting the invaders or were killed off by the diseases the Europeans brought with them. The fury of Western expansionism unleashed one of the worst cases of genocide in the history of modern civilization. At the time of the "Discovery," there were millions of natives in the

Brazil; less than 10 percent survived. Today there are about 250,000 Indians, made up of some 200 tribes. More than one-third of the tribes that existed have died off completely.

While the European conquerors exploited the land for profit, indigenous people have had a very spiritual relationship to the land. They live from the forest but they allow the jungle's flora and fauna to reproduce themselves. Indian leader Ailton Krenak says that Indians don't see the forest as a bunch of wild trees, but as a place where their history and future is written, a place to remember their dead and to provide for their sons and daughters. For them, the land is not a commodity; it is a sacred place. In the indigenous view of the world, the land doesn't belong to people; it's people who belong to the land.

Today, Indians are still being driven from their land. When the generals responsible for the coup in the 1960s decided they would "flood the Amazon with civilization," they unleashed a new wave of violence against the Indians. The government created tax incentives that encouraged cattle ranchers to clear the forest and establish pastures. This encouraged the ranchers to steal huge tracts of land from the Indians. New roads were built through the Amazon, but instead of helping the Indians, these new roads made it easier for outsiders to invade their territory. Thousands and thousands of *garimpeiros,* or miners, flooded Indian lands in search of gold, bringing environmental destruction and a new round of deadly diseases.

One of the Indian tribes most affected by the *garimpeiros* was the Yanomami. With about 20,000 people, the Yanomami represent one of the largest Indian nations in the Americas. It is one of the few tribes that until recently had no contact with the outside world and so had been able to maintain its cultural traditions. But the arrival of the *garimpeiros* in the 1980s changed all that. The miners infected the Yanomami with malaria, measles, polio, river blindness, and flu. Their traditional healers, *pajés,* were unable to cure these new diseases and thousands died.

In addition to the diseases, many Yanomami have been killed by *garimpeiros* in land conflicts. In 1993 a shocking massacre occurred in one of their villages. Dozens of men, women, and children were slaughtered, some decapitated with machetes. The Yanomami have been denouncing the destruction of their communities for decades. As their leader Davi Yanomami said, "When the whites came, many Indians turned into *urubutheri* — people who don't know how to hunt or fish, people who eat the leftovers from the plates of white people. They forget how to collect fruit from the trees, they forget our customs, they forget our language."

Many indigenous people who've been expelled from their land have become nomads, roaming around in search of a job and a place to live. Some become rural workers, hiring themselves out as cheap day laborers on the plantations or in the sugar and alcohol factories. Others find odd jobs in the city, living in shacks in the *favelas* and abandoning their traditional culture.

Another group that has been severely impacted by the invasion of its territory is the Kaiowá-Guarani. Many men have had to leave home in search of jobs, resulting in the break up of families, alcoholism and the loss of cultural identity. Some young Kaiowá-Guarani have become so desperate that they have resorted to suicide. A tragic number of Indians under the age of 20 have committed suicide in recent years. In 1995 alone, there were 50 such cases of suicides among the Kaiowá-Guarani in the state of Mato Grosso do Sul.

A congressional delegation visited the Kaiowá-Guarani to investigate this alarming rate of suicide. They brought back heart-wrenching stories of young boys and girls who took their own lives. In one family, a 13-year-old girl killed herself in 1992 and then in 1995 her 17-year-old brother hung himself from a tree by a pair of jeans. Suicide is not a traditional practice among the Kaiowá-Guarani. They consider it a disease that comes when people lose their traditional faith.

It's impossible for indigenous people to preserve their traditional ways without large tracts of land for hunting and for rotating their subsistence crops. That's why I get so mad when I hear people say that the Indians have too much land. They say it doesn't make sense to reserve so much land for so few Indians. But it's really the white ranchers who have too much land, not the Indians.

The Indians don't want charity or paternalism from the government. They want their leaders to have a chance to dialogue with government officials as equals. They don't want to be seen as children incapable of taking care of themselves. They have a long, rich tradition of organizing themselves into self-sustaining communities.

They also don't want us to romanticize their supposed "primitive state." The idea that native people were in some stagnant state before they came into contact with white people is not true. They have been constantly evolving, and most are not necessarily hostile to development or new technologies. The indigenous people want to improve their lives, but in a way that preserves their culture. They want schools that integrate modern learning with indigenous wisdom, and health care that combines Western medicine with herbal remedies.

Indians want their full rights as citizens and they have been organizing to get those rights. In 1980 the *União das Nações Indígenas* or Indigenous People's Union was formed. The union became skilled in lobbying for indigenous rights and coordinating advocacy groups concerned with native rights. For the first time in Brazil's history, they managed to push through a constitutional amendment that guaranteed the right of indigenous people to maintain their land, their organizations, their customs, languages, beliefs, and traditions. It also stated that any development of mining or dams affecting the indigenous people would require congressional approval, with indigenous participation in any decision. Brazil was recognized internationally for these great advances in protecting indigenous rights.

The Constitution also required that all the indigenous lands had to be demarcated by 1993. But by the time the date came, only about half the land had been protected because much of it was still in dispute. The large landowners, with powerful allies in Congress, had been trying to stop the demarcation process, and to roll back the constitutional guarantees. In 1996 they succeeding in having President Fernando Henrique Cardoso sign a new law allowing any person to dispute the ownership of indigenous land. This law is an outrage because it opens the door for ranchers and the mining and timber companies to once again invade Indian lands.

Another group that has been affected by the destruction of the forest is the *seringueiros,* or rubber tappers. Rubber tappers have lived and worked in the Amazon for over 100 years, extracting the liquid from the *seringueira,* or rubber tree. They were first brought to the Amazon by the rubber barons as slaves, and they were trained to fight against the Indians and drive them off their lands. In the 1970s, the government stopped giving subsidies to the rubber industry, and many companies closed down. The *seringueiros* were left in the Amazon, barely surviving. They began to organize their own cooperatives, but the expansion of cattle ranching threatened their livelihood by destroying the trees they needed to survive.

To protect the forests, the rubber tappers started using non-violent tactics like the *empate,* or stand-off. When they discovered that a cattle rancher was planning to destroy the forest to expand his landholding, they would peacefully occupy the land, along with their wives and children. They would talk with the ranchers' hired hands to try to convince them not to cut down the trees. In some cases, their presence would be enough to stop the destruction; other times, they'd be forcibly evicted, beaten up, and arrested.

When I was a deputy and we were working on the 1988 Constitution, the rubber tappers proposed and won the creation of *reservas extrativistas,* extractive reserves. Extractive reserves are legally protected tracts of rain forest from which only sustainably harvested forest products can be extracted. These include rubber, nuts, resins, and fruits. While slash and burn agriculture, cattle ranching and logging all entail clearing massive areas of forest, extractive reserves produce economic gain without cutting or burning trees. It is a way for local people to earn an income from the land without destroying the forest, a way of combining conservation with economic development.

In the Senate, I continue working for the rights of the forest people. I'm lucky to be able to work with another senator, Marina Silva, who is the main congressional spokesperson in defense of the Amazon. I have learned so much from Marina. We identify closely with each other because we are among the few senators who come from humble backgrounds and had very difficult lives. Marina's father was a poor rubber tapper and she worked with him in the forest from the time she was a child. When she was 16, she became terribly ill with hepatitis and almost died. Her family sent her to the city to get treatment at a free Catholic hospital. When she recovered, she began to work as a maid. Barely literate, she pushed herself to go to school in the evenings, and went all the way to the university. Then she met rubber tapper Chico Mendes, and they worked together to organize the *seringueiros* into a union.

Marina always talks with great affection about her friend Chico Mendes. He was a leader who won lots of international awards for his work to protect the rain forest while providing a sustainable living for the rubber tappers. But his efforts to organize the workers infuriated the big landowners. So did Chico's relentless denunciations of the ranchers' destruction of the forest and their violent attacks against rural workers. Chico Mendes was a thorn in the ranchers' side, and they longed to get rid of him.

On many occasions, Chico talked about the ranchers' attempts to kill him. He even mentioned the names of Darly and Darcy Alves, and gave proof to the authorities that these two ranchers were plotting to kill him. But the local police never did anything. In fact, those same ranchers had been convicted of killing two other rubber tappers, but they had escaped from jail with the help of the local police.

Chico's wife Ilzamar was also very worried. When they celebrated his forty-fourth birthday, he hugged her and said that it would probably be his last birthday they'd celebrate together. A week later, as Chico was walking toward his outhouse to take a shower, he was shot in the back and killed. Because of the international uproar over his death, the ranchers who shot him were arrested, but once again they escaped from jail and it was only years later that the police found them.

For Chico Mendes, the environment was not an academic field of study, it was his life. Many university-trained environmentalists are only concerned about trees, rivers, and clean air. Chico, in addition to defending the trees and the rivers and the air, defended the people of the Amazon. He helped create an alliance between the Indians and the rubber tappers. He also defended poor peasants and spoke out in favor of agrarian reform. That's why he was killed.

Throughout Brazilian history, all attempts to redistribute the land have been repressed. In the 1960s, there was a strong peasant movement calling for reform and when President Goulart took office in 1961, he promised a massive land reform program. His commitment to agrarian reform was one of the key reasons he was overthrown by a military coup in 1964.

Without a better distribution of land, there will never be a solution to the hunger and misery that wrack our nation. It doesn't make any sense for people to go hungry in a country like Brazil, which has the potential to feed all of Latin America. Brazil spends billions of dollars a year importing food, while less than 20 percent of our agricultural land is being used.

The small and medium farmers around the country have a relatively small portion of land, and get little government support. But they are the ones responsible for growing practically all the food we eat.

The vast majority of land in Brazil is in the hands of the huge landowners, the *latifundiários*. They make up just one percent of the population, but own practically half of Brazil's agricultural land. We have farms so big that they cover more land than some European countries! The *latifundiários* have taken over vast quantities of land in order to produce goods for export, or merely for speculation. With huge rates of inflation in the 1970s and 1980s, land was considered a safe investment.

Under Brazilian law, when ranchers want to claim untitled lands, they have to clear half the area as evidence of effective use. It's ironic to call cattle ranching an effective use of the land. It destroys the soil within 10 years, and leaves the land totally unusable for agriculture. It creates almost no jobs and very little food.

For the ranchers, the surest way to claim land is to clear as large an area as quickly as possible. So millions of acres of forest are reduced to dust each year, causing the massive migration of forest people. Today there are millions of heads of cattle grazing in the Amazon.

Another group vying for land in the Amazon are the settlers who came mainly from the impoverished northeast in the 1960s in the hopes of becoming small farmers. Millions of poor settlers migrated there, enticed by government promises of land and credit. But between the poor Amazon soil and lack of infrastructure, these settlers often found they could sell their land titles for more money than they could make from farming. Others had their land stolen by the ranchers and speculators. Today we have about 15 million rural people who are landless. Most of them are day laborers who work for little pay, and they can only find jobs at harvest time.

Some of these laborers work under the most miserable conditions imaginable. I recently read a study showing that 60,000 people work in virtual slave-like conditions in the fields. A labor recruiter goes to a poor town with high unemployment and gives the men an advance payment to entice them to work on the *latifúndios.* After they arrive, they realize they must not only pay back the advance but also pay for their food, drinks and even medicines—all at grossly inflated prices—which makes it impossible for them to ever pay their debts. They are watched by armed guards 24 hours a day, and locked up at night.

Other landless people have become *garimpeiros,* or miners. These miners are often seen as the bad guys, invading Indian lands and polluting the environment with the mercury that they use in the mining process. It's true that they are causing tremendous damage to the environment, but we should understand that the *garimpeiros* are themselves victims of Brazilian poverty. They gravitate to the mines because the rural wages are so low and they can't find jobs in the cities. They are usually very poor and their working conditions are deplorable.

Many of the landless migrate to the big cities to look for a way to survive. In the past two decades, more Brazilians have migrated from the countryside to the city than the entire population of Argentina! With such miserable conditions in the countryside, it's no wonder that there is a massive rural exodus.

In the 1970s, church activists began organizing the Pastoral Land Commission to demand justice in the countryside. But over the years, life has only gotten worse for the rural poor. Inflation and land speculation have increased the value of farmland, pushing over a million rural workers off the land each year since the 1960s.

Today, the major group fighting for land is the *Movimento Sem Terra,* the Landless Workers Movement. Since its founding in 1985, it has forced the government to expropriate hundreds of thousands of acres of idle land all over the country. The Constitution allows for the expropriation of unused land to benefit landless peasants. But the people in power are not interested in enforcing this law. There is a large land-owning bloc in Congress, and in most towns, the big landowners help elect local politicians and have control of the police.

So the Landless Workers Movement has to force the government to redistribute the land. It organizes peasant families to occupy unused land that belongs to rich owners who live in the cities and use their property for tax write-offs. The time and place of the occupation is unknown to all but a handful of the top organizers until the last minute. Then, the families pour onto the land and set up camp. In the best of cases, the occupation forces the government to step in and begin negotiations to turn the land over to the peasants. In the worst of cases, the owners send in the police and their private armies to evict them. Since the 1964 military coup, almost 2,000 rural workers and activists have been killed in struggles over land, and virtually none of the killers have been punished.

In 1995, there was a bloody clash in the state of Rondônia, when the police stormed a land occupation carried out by some 600 families. It was horrible. The police arrived in the dark at about 4 am, and without warning began shooting indiscriminately at men, women, and children. They killed 11 people, including a seven-year-old girl who was shot in the back while running away. The police were barbaric—they beat people viciously, burned down their tents and raped women. More than 1,000 people were wounded. I heard parts of their testimonies, and it was heart-breaking. The cruelty of the police was unbelievable! One boy was forced to eat the brains of his dead companion; a man was forced to drink his dead friend's blood.

Despite the horrendous violation of human rights, none of the policemen involved has been convicted. A few months later, Manoel Ribeiro, a city council member who was helping to investigate the massacre, was shot in front of his house in full view of his pregnant wife.

In 1996, another brutal massacre occurred in Eldorado dos Carajás, in the state of Pará, when the military police attacked a peaceful demonstration of about 2,000 men, women and children who are part of the Landless Workers Movement. Hundreds of heavily armed police officers surrounded the demonstrators, and began throwing tear gas bombs into the crowd. Then they started shooting to kill, aiming right at the people's heads and chests. The police picked out the leaders of the movement, and murdered eight of them right on the spot. In the end, a total of 19 people were killed and dozens were wounded.

It has taken so many years of struggle and so many deaths for the international community to pay attention to these violent land conflicts in Brazil. But it is mainly the human rights organizations that have been concerned about this issue. Unfortunately, many of the environmental groups fail to make the connections between the need to preserve the environment and the needs of the people who are trying to live off the land.

In the past few decades there has been a surge of environmentalists worldwide who are concerned about the future of the Amazon. They talk about preserving the flora of the Amazon because it is the "lungs of the planet" or preserving particular animals because they are endangered. But they often forget that the Amazon is also the stomach of the forest people. The ecological question has to take into consideration the survival of people as well. For example, for some indigenous groups, alligator has always been a part of their traditional diet. They don't kill alligators to make purses and shoes for export; they eat alligator to survive. You can't just say to these people, "Stop eating alligators because they're an endangered species." We have to respect the culture and needs of the people who live in the forest.

This "green wave" of international environmentalists intent on saving Brazil really picked up force in the 1980s, when satellite photos showed massive fires raging all over the Amazon. Sometimes there were over 5,000 fires burning at one time, and the smoke was so thick that pilots couldn't land on the Amazon's airstrips. These images shocked the world, and some environmentalists even had the nerve to suggest that the Amazon be placed under the supervision of the United Nations.

We in Brazil often get the impression that the First World wants to preserve the forests of the Third World, but for its own benefit. This became clear during the negotiations of recent world trade agreements. The United States threatened to impose sanctions against Brazil if we didn't allow multinational corporations to register patents for any plants or animals from our forest. With these patents, pharmaceutical companies would own the rights to use these natural resources, without giving compensation to the people of the forest. It's really outrageous. They're saying to us, "Preserve your resources so we can profit from them and give you nothing in return."

What's even more outrageous is that while the people in the North are crying about the Amazon, they're cutting down their own forests and continuing the destructive lifestyles that are at the root of environmental devastation. As long as the industrialized countries refuse to protect their own environment and stop their overconsumption, many people in Brazil will see their concern for preserving our resources as a form of ecological imperialism.

I'm not saying we don't need international support for preserving our forests. We do. And I believe that people all over the world could benefit from the amazing biodiversity that Brazil has to offer. But you can't save the trees and the plants and the animals without saving the people. And you can't save the people without democratizing the land.

Chapter Eight
We, Too, Are the Children of Brazil

"Why have so many people become indifferent to the pain of our street children?"

Photo by Jorge Nunes

É bota de sete léguas
caminhando pelo chão.
Pé inchado, descalço,
doído
às vezes ferido
mas que conhece a vida
isso conhece.
Pé de moleque danado,
levado da breca,
corre pelas ruas,
salta como pererreca.
Dá dó vê pé de moleque
no piso ardente
engraxar sapatos
de quem tem.
Eta, pé de moleque
moleque de pé
dá prazer
ver a coragem
em você.

You travel for miles on end
your feet on the ground
swollen, barefoot
in pain
sometimes hurt
but you know life
yes, that you know.
Feet of a naughty kid
mischievous
running through the streets
jumping like a tree frog.
It's sad to see your feet
on the burning ground
shining shoes
for those who have.
Yes, your feet
standing tall
It's so good
to see such courage
in you.

—Benedita da Silva

The hardships of my youth will always be with me, and that's why I'm so anguished when I see abused or abandoned children, children who are hungry, children who have to work when they should be at school. I know how it feels, I've been there.

We need to stop and think about what it means to be a child or an adolescent in Brazil today. I'm not talking about the conventional image you see on TV commercials every day, of beautiful, white children who are well dressed and well fed. I'm not talking about adolescents whose main concern is what's hip in music and fashion, kids who hang out in shopping malls and take vacations in Disneyland.

I'm talking about the children and adolescents who live on the margins, who are the victims of violence. The children who are illegally adopted, raped, and beaten, exploited like slaves for their labor. This is the painful reality of millions of young people in Brazil today. There are 35 million young people living in misery, and seven million of them live on the streets.

These street children are called all sorts of pejorative names: *pivete,* thief; *trombadinha,* pickpocket; *maloqueiro,* street delinquent; *menor,* juvenile delinquent; and *marginal,* criminal.

Another term that people use is *abandonado,* abandoned. According to the dictionary, abandoned means forsaken, neglected, deserted. Many people believe that street children have been abandoned by their families because they're bad kids. This implies that it's the kids' fault and absolves other sectors of society or the state of their responsibility. But these kids are not out on the streets because their families have abandoned them; they're out of the street because an entire social class has been abandoned by the rest of society.

Who are these so-called "abandoned children" we see sleeping in park benches, under bridges and in bus stations? It's true that some of these kids leave their homes because they were beaten and mistreated by a family member, like their fathers, uncles or older brothers. Some girls have been sexually abused by family members, or by their mothers' boyfriends, and run away. For these kids, the street represents freedom.

But in many cases, these street kids did not leave home because of abusive parents. They leave home because of poverty. These kids who are apparently "alone in the world" usually maintain ties with their families and contribute to the family's income. In some cases, they are the family's sole source of support.

The street children go out during the day to look for some kind of work. They sell popsicles or candies, shine shoes, carry grocery bags, clean windshields or collect cardboard. Some continue to go home at night to sleep. Others find it difficult to return home every day because they don't have money for the bus fare, so they end up sleeping on the streets. But they still maintain their obligation to help their families, and they still go back home from time to time.

I had the opportunity to talk to many of these kids when I participated in congressional investigations on street children. We listened to dozens of testimonies from the children themselves. Let me just pull one of them out so you can hear them in their own words. A boy named José da Silva says:

"I ended up in the street when I was six years old, because my family was so poor and I had to work. I started meeting other kids in the city and sleeping out on the street because it was so far to go back home at night. Little by little, I became addicted to life on the streets. Sometimes we worked, sometimes we had to beg or steal because we were hungry."

"There are people who say, 'We should just kill those punks. They stole my watch. They stole my wife's gold necklace.' They don't understand that we're hungry. And when we ask for food or money, they look at us like we're a piece of crap and say, 'Get lost.' So what else can we do?"

To make life on the streets more bearable, many children turn to drugs. Some of them told me that they sniff glue to forget about their hunger. More recently, drug dealers have involved the kids in the selling of drugs, and now more children have been using marijuana, cocaine, and crack. This has made street life even more dangerous. Let me read you this interview with one of the kids:

"Sometimes we'd fight among each other, especially when we sniffed glue or did other drugs. One day a friend of mine was shooting up with a few other guys. He had some money hidden in his shirt. When these guys saw the money, they gave my friend a double hit and he started shaking and foaming at the mouth. Then they beat him, stole the money, and left him dead."

News reports sensationalize thefts and violence committed by street children, and it creates a certain panic among the upper and middle classes. The rich don't pay any attention to these kids if they stay in the *favelas*. It's only when they go to the city centers, public parks and upper-class neighborhoods that it becomes a scandal. For the rich, the worst crime these children have committed is defying the segregated order of our cities.

One way of getting these children off the streets has been to round them up in police sweeps. Different cities have passed regulations saying that minors found begging or sleeping on the streets would be picked up and taken to state institutions. All over the country there have been these clean-up operations they call *Arrastão*, Operation Sweep Up, where the police indiscriminately round up hundreds of children.

I have strongly denounced these repressive measures. They violate the constitution by restricting the freedom of those who've committed no crime, except for the crime of being poor. Picking the children up off the streets is not even efficient, because there are no decent government programs to help them. So they end up right back on the street again.

In fact, the state institutions have been part of the problem. There is this network of institutions called *Fundação Estadual do Bem Estar do Menor,* State Foundation for the Well-Being of Minors, know as FEBEM. Instead of educating and helping the children, the people running these institutions abuse them. In our investigations, we found that the children were systematically subjected to physical and psychological torture. In one institution, the inspectors routinely beat the kids with a *chicote,* a whip, called *Peru de boi,* or bull's balls. We found numerous cases of children who were punched, kicked, and threatened with strangulation.

Listen to the testimony of one of the boys we interviewed:

"I was in and out of FEBEM about 50 times, because I got so good at escaping. Every time we went in, the first thing they'd do is give us five lashes as a punishment for *vadiagem,* vagrancy. The first time I went there I thought it was gonna be like a school and I would learn good things. But all I learned was how to fight and steal, and I'd get beat up all the time. At bedtime, the guards would go watch TV and leave the older kids in charge. When we were asleep, these guys would take rags full of dirt and rub them in our faces. We'd wake up screaming and crying, and the guards would come and beat us.

But if we fought among ourselves, the guards wouldn't stop the fight until the weaker guy was totally beaten, with his face all swollen and bloody. Once the guards punished some kids by locking them up in a small, dark room. The kids started to fight, and the guards didn't do anything about it. So one of the boys set a mattress on fire. When the guards finally opened the door, the kids were all burned and had to be rushed to the hospital."

These institutions had such a bad reputation that a number of them have been shut down. But the methods used to get rid of these street children have become even more violent. In recent years, Brazil has become known around the world for murdering street children.

On average, over four children are murdered every day in Brazil. Eighty percent of the street children murdered are black, and the majority are between 15 and 17 years old. In 1990 a common grave containing the bodies of over 500 children was discovered in a São Paulo cemetery.

When people hear about such atrocities, they naturally ask: "Who would do such a thing? What are their motives?" The assassins are often police officers who join *esquadrões da morte,* death squads, to augment their meager salaries. They usually come from the same poor neighborhoods as their victims. Some are paid by businesspeople to *"limpar a área,"* clean the area or *"passar o rodo,"* mop up. They cynically call themselves *justiceiros:* those who do justice.

These people kill for money, but they also believe the public is behind them. It's common to hear people make light of the murder of street children, saying things like *"Ao se matar um pivete, está se fazendo um bem para a sociedade"*—killing those little punks is good for society.

The first death squads in Brazil appeared during the military dictatorship in 1964. One famous group was called *Os Doze Homens de Ouro,* the Twelve Gold Men. It was made up of police officers and sheriffs who targeted so-called terrorists and subversives. One former member of that group is a state representative in Rio, José Guilherme Godinho, whose slogan was "A good criminal is a dead criminal."

This culture of violence and impunity created within the police forces remained even after the dictatorship. Our congressional study revealed that in Rio alone, there are 15 death squads that target children and work under the protection of the police and justice system. We found a whole network of people involved:

businessmen, active and retired policemen, merchants associations, high-ranking officers, security guards, lawyers, and judges.

In the last few years, the killings have gotten even worse with the influence of drug dealers. In fact, the majority of the killings are now drug related. The street kids have become the foot soldiers for the drug gangs, and more and more of them are killed off in turf wars.

The police and others involved in the murder of children act as both judge and executor. They hand down death sentences as if they had the moral right to decide who lives or dies. They usually kidnap the children, take them to an isolated place, and then shoot them. When they put their hands on the trigger, they already know that they won't be caught.

I was so indignant when I heard about the brutal murder a few months back of three girls from the Western Zone of Rio. The first victim was 13-year-old Daiane, who was violently raped and murdered. Then there was Jussara and Sandra Cristina, who were only 11 years old. There were strong indications that their murders were the work of the same person. But the police never even came close to identifying the assassin. According to Amnesty International, 90 percent of the killings of impoverished Brazilian children and adolescents have never been resolved.

The Brazilian media talks about violence against street children as if it were a normal and permanent feature of Brazilian society, and people have become indifferent to the children's pain. I remember the terrible, emotional images of a boat accident in the bay of Guanabara in 1988. A few hundred people were at a fancy New Year's party on the boat when it capsized. Over 50 people died. The news media carried detailed coverage of the rescue operations and all of Brazil was grief-stricken.

So why have Brazilians become so indifferent to the daily tragedy that affects our youth and kills so many more people than these kinds of accidents? This reminds me of a song by Milton

Nascimento and Ronaldo Bastos called *Menino*, or Boy, that says *"Quem cala sobre teu corpo consente na tua morte; talhada a ferro e fogo nas profundezas do corte; que a bala riscou no peito; quem cala morre contigo"* —Those who are silent facing your body are complicit in your death; carved with iron and fire in the depths of your skin, the bullet lodged in your chest; those who are silent die with you.

The first incident that really ignited public indignation was the Candelária Massacre in 1993. In the dead of the night, eight children were gunned down as they slept near the Candelária Church in downtown Rio. It was the first time that people mobilized and took to the streets to protest these killings.

The massacre was denounced by human rights groups all over the world, and they put a lot of pressure on the Brazilian government to take action. Finally, three years later, a policeman was convicted for taking part in the massacre. During the trial, Brazilians were shocked to hear his justification for the murders: it was because the children had thrown stones at a police car the day before. The only surviving boy willing to testify described how three police officers had grabbed him and several of his friends, beat them viciously and shoved them into a car. Then he was shot in the head, dumped on the side of the road and left for dead.

The conviction of this policeman is a positive step in bringing human rights abusers to justice. It's very important because it marks the beginning of the end of impunity for the police.

In this case and in all of our work around street children, we have come to realize the importance of international support. The sad truth is that it's only when the international community gets involved that the Brazilian government responds. The same is true of our media. Brazilian human rights groups have been trying for years to get more media attention about these horrendous killings. But they had to first get the foreign press to cover the issue. Only then did the Brazilian press give it greater coverage.

Another form of child abuse that gets little attention is child labor. In Brazil, children begin to work as early as six or seven years old. They often have to take on the role of breadwinner, with their parents unemployed or absent. The majority of young people don't have work permits, so they have no guaranteed rights. They get miserable wages for long hours of work, and these children account for about 60 percent of work accidents. The International Labor Organization said that it's difficult to find a commodity made in Brazil that doesn't have the mark of child labor stamped on it.

Some of the worst conditions are in the rural areas. In this "modern age," child workers in the *carvoarias,* the coal pits, work 14 hours a day in slave-like conditions, without boots, gloves or protective masks. They sleep on cardboard beds in crowded dormitories with no air circulation. Children work in similar conditions in the cane fields and sugar factories.

Many of these kids are recruited as day workers by labor contractors known as *gatos,* or cats. When the children get to the *fazenda* to start work, they're already in debt because they have to pay for transportation, room, and board. The *gatos* take their wages to pay off their expenses. That's how the children get caught up in an endless cycle of debt. They are not free to leave until the debt is paid off.

Girls also get caught in this devious web of abuse. Labor contractors recruit poor girls with promises of work as waitresses, cooks, and dishwashers in restaurants in the Amazon, where the miners work. Then they end up being forced into prostitution. These girls become the property of a network of brothels that keep them enslaved through debt bondage and make lots of money off their plight.

I learned a lot about this issue of child prostitution during a congressional investigation we did in 1993. Our findings were shocking. We estimated that there are about 500,000 under-age prostitutes in the country—that's one out of every 300 Brazilians! We uncovered and denounced a host of horrors—rapes, physical and psychological violence within the home, boys and girls who prostitute themselves for a sandwich or a plate of food, girl prostitutes who are virtual slaves of the gold miners in the north or in hotels in the south and southeast, unwanted pregnancies, life-threatening abortions, police brutality, sexually-transmitted diseases, illegal international adoptions, girls addicted to drugs and alcohol, the spread of AIDS, the practice of pedophilia, the use of children in pornographic films for export.

We found a growing number of children involved in sex tourism, especially in the cities of the northeast. International travel agencies sell Brazil as a place where sex is cheap and easy, with brochures showing nude or semi-nude bodies in beautiful beach settings.

Child prostitution is particularly a problem among street children. A study done by a non-governmental group in Recife called *Casa de Passagem,* House of Passage, found that 44 percent of street girls lived off prostitution. The majority left home when they were under 16, sometimes as young as six years old.

The study found that girls are leaving home at an earlier and earlier age, but they don't last very long on the streets. At the age of 16, they're already considered veterans. By the time they're 20, they're used up and replaced by younger girls. The longest they stay on the street is usually about 10 years. After that, they have few options. They might end up in prison or in shelters. They might be murdered or kill themselves. Or they're permanently scarred and go through life "psychologically dead."

Educators who work with these girls find that they suffer from a tremendous lack of self-esteem. It's easy to see why—they're at the bottom of the social order. They are poor, mostly black women who are seen as not only prostitutes but criminals. They are also victims of police violence, even more so than the boys because of sexual abuse. The street boys take advantage of the girls as well.

The constant humiliation they suffer leads them to self-destructive acts, such as cutting themselves with knives and razor blades. Sometimes they're trying to prove how tough they are. The toughest girls are the ones with the most scars. Other times it's just the opposite, it's a call for help. At the very least they might end up in a hospital where someone will take care of them.

Many of these girls get desperate when they get pregnant and have no way to support their babies. Some willingly give their babies up for adoption, but in recent years there are more and more cases of babies being stolen from poor women as part of a sinister international network of illegal adoption.

The majority of the babies are being sent to Italy, France, and Canada. The babies are taken out of Brazil with false passports. The illegal export of babies is a lucrative business; I've heard that the traffickers can get $25,000 to $30,000 per baby. There are 4,000 police stations in Brazil that have filed reports of children disappearing mysteriously. There have been many cases of children disappearing from hospitals and we suspect that some hospital workers might be involved in this trafficking of babies.

These disappearances have fueled rumors that an even more sinister network might exist, a network in which babies are illegally exported overseas, where their organs are used for transplants. We know that there is a strong demand for these organs overseas and few regulations. But it was impossible for us to find any concrete proof because the hospitals that perform these transplants have a strict code of medical confidentiality about the origin of the organs.

We recommended that the government undertake a more thorough investigation into this organ business and implement stronger controls over foreign adoptions. In the meantime, there is now a civic group formed by the parents themselves called the National Movement in Defense of Disappeared Children that tries to solve individual cases and pressure the government for stricter regulations on adoptions.

This issue of adoption, even legal adoption, is very complex. Some parents realize that the circumstances of their lives don't allow them to raise their children. In these cases, I think they should have the right to give their babies up for adoption. But adoption can't be used as a solution to poverty; and certainly no one should be able to force poor mothers to give up custody of their children.

There are many people who encourage adoption as a way to help families who can't afford to raise their children. Congress has passed bills that give benefits to these adoptive families, such as tax breaks, food stamps, and so on. But I'm not in favor of these measures because I think they have it backwards. Instead of giving benefits to the people who adopt, we should give benefits to the biological parents to make it easier for them to keep their own children. The adoptive parents think they're doing a good thing, but adoption only relieves the state of its responsibility to look out for the well-being of the nation's children and to help out needy parents.

When I think about the tragic condition of so many Brazilian children, I ask myself why this is happening in Brazil and not in other poor countries. I've traveled to China, I've traveled to other countries in Latin America, and I've seen a lot of poverty. But I don't see the same cruelty inflicted on young people.

I suppose we have to look back to the time of slavery. The 1870 *Lei do Ventre Livre,* Law of the Free Womb, was a very contradictory law. Yes, it gave freedom to young slaves, but by separating free children from their enslaved parents, it ended up depriving the children of the right to live with their parents, kicking them out on the streets, and leaving them with nothing to guarantee their survival. In the end, the Law of the Free Womb was nothing more than the official abandonment of black children.

Colonization also brought us an economic model that created a huge gap between rich and poor. The increasing concentration of wealth means that today the fancy restaurants along Rio's beaches are full of well-to-do customers while the sidewalks outside are full of hungry children.

Despite the fact that infant mortality rates in Brazil have gone down in the past decade, the statistics are still appalling. The majority of deaths are caused by easily preventable diseases, such as diarrhea and respiratory infections. Thirty percent of children under five suffer from some kind of malnutrition, and it is estimated that 800 children die every day from hunger-related diseases.

Look at education. Of every 100 children that enter elementary school, just 22 make it to eighth grade. According to UNICEF, the drop-out rate in Brazil is surpassed by only two countries: Guinea Bissau and Haiti. A country that doesn't believe in or invest in its youth is a country that doesn't have a future.

But what gives me hope is to see how many people have been organizing at the grassroots level in recent years. In the early 1980s, a number of children's rights organizations and the progressive Catholic Church formed a network of alternative programs to assist street children. They rejected the government's repressive approach, which only created a cycle of violence. They also rejected the paternalistic "assistance model" of child welfare favored by some international organizations. Instead, they created alternative programs with a very different approach.

Their approach is not to lock children up in institutions, but to engage the children in creating support services that best fit their needs. This might take the form of job training, cultural activities, literacy classes, counseling, or health services. Some organizations provide overnight shelter, but the kids are free to come and go.

In 1985 this network created an umbrella organization called the *Movimento Nacional dos Meninos e Meninas de Rua,* the National Movement of Street Children. In addition to its headquarters in Brasília, the movement has offices all over Brazil. While social workers and educators have been involved with the movement, the main force has been the street children themselves. About 3,000 youth activists are officially affiliated with the movement.

In our interviews with street kids during our congressional study, we discovered the tremendous impact the movement has had on the children's lives. Let me give you an example:

"When I was in the streets, I thought life was like a war, and we couldn't trust anybody. Then I got to know the movement and it taught me a lot. I'd go to the meetings and hear the stories of others like me. I began to see that all of us are important in life, and that the government and the rich should treat us like human beings. The movement taught me that we have rights that must be respected."

You can really understand the philosophy of this movement when you go to one of their national meetings. You don't see a group of adults sitting around in a fancy conference hall talking about what's best for the children. You see children themselves talking about what's best for them. Adults are present in these meetings, but they are asked to remain silent. The spotlight is on the young people.

In their meetings, the children talk about everything from AIDS to legislation to police conduct. No matter what the topic, there is always a cultural component: music, dance, theater, *capoeira,* mask making, acrobatics. They also write beautiful poems. This one is one of my favorites:

Para vocês vida bela,	For you, the good life
Para nós, favela	For us, the *favela*
Para vocês avião,	For you, the airplane
Para nós, camburão	For us, the paddy wagon
Para vocês carros do ano,	For you, the latest model car
Para nós, resto de pano	For us, the scrap heap
Para vocês piscina,	For you, the swimming pool
Para nós, chacina	For us, the blood bath
Para vocês escola,	For you, learning
Para nós, pedir esmola.	For us, begging
Para vocês ir à Lua,	For you, going to the moon
Para nós, morar na rua	For us, living on the street
Para vocês Coca-Cola,	For you, Coca-Cola
Para nós, cheirar cola	For us, sniffing glue
Para vocês luxo,	For you, a big bash
Para nós, lixo	For us, the trash
Para vocês tá bom, felicidade,	For you, your own happiness
Para nós, igualdade.	For us, the fight for equity
Para vocês imobiliária,	For you, real estate
Para nós, reforma agrária.	For us, a piece of land
Para vocês exploração,	For you, exploitation
Para nós, libertação.	For us, liberation
Nós também queremos viver!	We, too, want to live!

I remember the time the movement organized a demonstration in which hundreds of street children took over Congress to present their demands. They came in colorful costumes, dancing and singing, and they made powerful speeches. It's so moving to see how motivated and creative they are, despite the hardships they face in their everyday life.

One of the main goals of the movement has been to pass legislation that protects children. To come up with the draft document, they held thousands of meetings across the country seeking input and support. In 1990 they were successful in getting Congress to pass the Child and Adolescent Act, which is one of the most radical children's rights statutes in the world.

This act is an extremely comprehensive document in which children's rights are spelled out in extensive detail. It guarantees children's access to health care, housing, and education, and the right to use public spaces. It makes it illegal for minors under 14 to work, except as apprentices, and it calls for job training and education programs.

The act states that children's welfare should be a priority in government policy. But the most innovative piece of this legislation is that it places child welfare policy in the hands of grassroots councils rather than governmental institutions. These councils are highly decentralized bodies that include representatives of the children themselves and non-governmental advocacy organizations.

Since the passage of the Child and Adolescent Act, the children's movement seems to be gaining public support. Their message is a simple but poignant one. These are *our* children, and we are collectively responsible for them. As one child said:

"Our crime is to live on the streets, our crime is that we're poor. Should we pay with our lives? We would like to sleep on clean sheets and have warm blankets. We would like to play and have fun. We would like to go to school. Aren't these things you give to your own precious children? Well, we are your children, too, because we are the children of Brazil."

Chapter Nine
Time to Cut Up the Pie

Benedita, on a visit to South Africa, meets with President Nelson Mandela

I will no longer accept any argument for the perpetuation of hunger. I won't accept any economic policy or theory that tries to justify, rationalize, or make us accept hunger and misery as a natural, human fact.

> —Herbert "Betinho" de Souza,
> Brazil's foremost anti-hunger
> activist, died in 1997.

I'm not a trained economist and like most people, I used to feel that economic issues were abstract and disconnected from my everyday life. When experts talk about the economy, they use a lot of technical terms that make people feel that these concepts are just too complicated. That's why many people don't even bother trying to understand economic policies. They prefer to leave it to the experts, thinking that they have the answers.

I get really upset when economists and politicians use technical language to confuse and manipulate people. When we hear that the economy is growing, it gives the impression that everyone is working, happy, and healthy. But these numbers don't reflect the daily reality of our lives. Sure, there's a segment of society that's doing well, but they're certainly not the majority. All too often those in power use economic figures to defend their own interests, and to perpetuate the notion of wise men and fools, the ones who give orders and the ones who obey. All these numbers, all these charts and data—most of it is meaningless.

I don't need to be an economist to know that with three percent of our gross domestic product, we could solve the housing problem in all the *favelas* in five years. I don't need to be an economist to understand that some products are cheaper because they are made with child labor. I don't need to be an economist to understand why so many people in Brazil are hungry. We don't need lots of charts and numbers; what we need is a government and a budget that give priority to social programs.

Look at some of the ridiculous explanations these economic "experts" have for why there's so much hunger and poverty in Brazil. Some say the workers' salaries are too high to be competitive on the world market. Others blame it on overpopulation. Others say the state is too spendthrift, wasting money on social programs. But you don't have to be an expert to understand the real reason for the increasing impoverishment of the Brazilian people: the present economic model.

This model, called neoliberalism, is based on blind faith in the free market. It believes that the market will automatically solve our economic and social ills, and calls for minimum levels of government intervention. Enterprises like telecommunications and the oil industry that have been in the hands of the state should be sold off to private owners. Regulations that protect national companies, as well as tariffs that make it more difficult for foreign products to enter Brazil, should be lifted. And social programs should be cut in order to balance the budget and pay back the huge loans we owe to foreign banks.

This packet of economic policies is imposed on Third World countries by international financial institutions like the International Monetary Fund, the World Bank, and the Club of Paris. They tell poor countries like Brazil that we can only get loans if we follow those policies.

It is an economic model that reverses the efforts made by many Third World nations during the 1960s and 1970s to create domestic industries. Until recently, many countries had strong regulations to protect our internal markets. Since the 1980s, we've all been under intense pressure from the international financial institutions to lift these regulations and open our economies to the world market.

In the neoliberal system, the market is supposed to resolve everything, but it certainly doesn't resolve the biggest problem we face, which is how to bridge the enormous gap between the haves and the have nots. In Brazil we have the super-rich, who live better than the rich in wealthy countries. They have their sumptuous mansions, country clubs, and beach houses, where they are waited on hand and foot by an army of maids and butlers. They go on weekend shopping sprees to Miami, they send their children to the best European schools, and they have chummy relationships with top government officials. On the other side of paradise are Brazilians who can't feed their children, who have no access to the halls of power, and for whom the capitalist dream is a cruel joke.

According to the United Nations, Brazil has the worst income gap between the rich and poor in the entire world! How shameful it is to be the world champions of inequality. The entire bottom half of Brazilian society receives less than four percent of the national income, while the richest 10 percent get over 50 percent of the income! Compare this to countries like Sweden, Belgium, and Holland, where the richest 10 percent of the population receives only 20 percent of the income.

In all the phases of our history since the time of colonialism, economic growth never benefited the majority of the population. That's because our governments have always been unwilling to touch the colossal appetites of the bankers, the financial speculators, the landowners, or the big businessmen. In Brazil, governments come and go, but the social divisions remain intact. When times are bad, it's the poor who have to tighten their belts. When times are good, it's the rich who profit.

During the military dictatorship, the generals tried to justify this social injustice by saying, *"Primeiro o bolo precisa crescer para depois ser dividido,"* —first the pie has to grow so we can divide it later. After 20 years of military rule, Brazil emerged in the 1980s as one of the world's top 10 economies, a success story among third world nations. But the pie was never divided. The "economic miracle" benefited the few at the expense of the many.

The new civilian governments have maintained strong ties with the same economic elites. With all their blah-blah-blah about social justice, the only concrete social programs they have implemented follow a paternalistic, populist formula that gives charity to the poor as a way to keep them quiet and submissive.

Despite our nation's vast resources, none of our governments has been able to take Brazil out of its Third World status. Today, the rich countries tell us that if we want to grow and prosper, we have to open up our markets. But if you look back at the history of countries like Japan and the United States, you see that they created strong economies by protecting their own markets. Even today, now that they have become the strongest economies in the world and the most vociferous advocates of "free trade," they still maintain government subsidies to national industries and other protectionist policies. For example, the United States gives huge subsidies to its farmers, who then export cheap grain overseas and undercut Latin producers.

Brazil has been trying to build a high-tech sector—computers, satellites, biotechnology, optics—but it has been under pressure from the U.S. for years to stop protecting its high-tech industry and open up to U.S. exports. Meanwhile, the U.S. government has heavily subsidized its own high-tech industry by providing billions in research. In the 1990s, Brazil caved in to U.S. pressure to stop protecting its computer industry, and since then the imports have flooded in.

So when the rich countries tell us to open our markets, they are saying, "Do as I say, not as I do." From my point of view, what they really want is open access to our internal markets and resources so they can continue to profit at our expense.

Instead of being honest and saying, "Whether you like it or not, there's a new global order and we, the elites and the multinationals, will decide who eats and who doesn't," they say, "There are inexorable laws of the free market we must all adhere to. And don't worry, if the free market is left to perform its miracles, all these nasty social problems will be solved."

Since I've been in public office, it's become clear to me just how hypocritical this free market talk is. Publicly, the big business community calls for the government to stay out of the way and let the private sector take charge. Privately, they are always asking the government for handouts—state financing, loan guarantees, inflated government contracts, monopoly licenses.

Leaving economic growth solely in the hands of market forces will never guarantee social equilibrium and equity. The state has to play a major role in trying to harmonize the different social forces. On one side are the business people who are out to defend their own interests and profits, regardless of the needs of the rest of society. On the other side are the impoverished masses, the ones who create the wealth but don't share in the profits. And in the middle is the state, which is supposed to curb capitalism's worst excesses and steer the economy in a direction that meets the needs of the majority of its citizens. The state is supposed to represent public, not private, interests.

The reforms being pushed on Third World countries include privatization, that is, the selling off of state-run enterprises to the private sector. But if you look at countries like Sweden, Denmark, and Switzerland, where there is a high standard of living across the board, you find that the state plays an active role in the economy. In some cases, the state controls as much as 40 percent of the economy. These countries prove that it's possible to have healthy and competitive relations between the public and private sectors, as long as the interests of the public come first.

Brazil has a history of state-run enterprises in key economic sectors, such as telecommunications, mining, and oil. It's true that the state's involvement in the economy has been marred by corruption and mismanagement. But before we condemn the whole notion of state enterprises, we have to look back at the history of these companies to understand why they've been so inefficient.

Many of the state enterprises were created during the military regime. They were turned over to generals, colonels, and their cronies as a way to line their pockets. They were not required to be profitable, so they could get away with being grossly inefficient. The administrators named by the military regime were responsible for the bankruptcy and mismanagement of mining companies and banks. They were so corrupt and inefficient that they left the impression among the general public that the Brazilian state doesn't have the capacity to run well-managed companies that can compete in the marketplace.

Today this critique of state enterprises is used to push public opinion into accepting the privatization of strategic sectors of our economy. The argument in favor of privatization is a simple one: state enterprises are inefficient, the private sector is efficient. So if we sell off our state enterprises to private companies the state will earn money from the sales, the companies will be better run and everyone will be happy.

All over the world, poor countries have been selling off their state enterprises. And what happens? They lose control of the most vital sectors of their economies to foreign companies or rich government cronies who buy them at rock bottom prices. And these companies—whose main objective is not to provide services to the local population but to make profits—often lay off workers, cut services, and run the companies into the ground. All over Latin America, the backlash against privatization has been growing. Workers, poor people, students, and civic groups have been protesting the selling off of key state enterprises.

In Brazil there is currently a pitched battle over Petrobrás, the 40-year-old, state-run oil industry, and the state-owned mining company Vale do Rio Doce. In 1992 Petrobrás won an international award as the oil company with the most advanced technology for exploration in the deep sea. Petrobrás has also invested more in Brazil than any foreign company, and in the last 20 years the government has not spent a dime to keep it running.

Vale do Rio Doce is one of the most important mining companies in the world. Its vast deposits of iron, manganese, gold, and bauxite represent an incalculable treasure for Brazil. It's also important for its railroads and shipping facilities. A large part of the company's profits has been going to support the nation's health and education systems.

Those in favor of privatization say the government should not be in the business of running an oil or a mining company. Then why do so many other countries keep these industries in state hands? It's not by chance that Arab countries keep strict state control over their oil industry. In an area so strategic and vital to the national interest, these countries prefer to control their key resources rather than sell them off to foreigners.

Besides, it's not as if these foreign oil companies are so efficient and are governed purely by market forces. No, they are giant cartels and oligopolies that set prices and control competition. A very small and extremely powerful group of gigantic companies keep a tight lid on the market and manipulate it to their advantage. Countries like Brazil can't afford to compromise our sovereignty to this great charade called "the market," which is always "free and open" in theory but closed and manipulated in reality.

Instead of taking the hard-line ideological position that privatization is good and state-run companies are bad, we should look at each enterprise on a case-by-case basis. Rather than advocating the wholesale dismantling of state-run industries, we should first try to improve those industries—root out corruption, attract good management, give the workers a greater say in running the industries, and create mechanisms for more public access and input. More democratic and efficient state-run companies should be able to provide good services to the population while bringing in much-needed state revenue.

The privatization of state industries is also a major blow to the unions, which have traditionally been strong in the state sector. In fact, the whole neoliberal model is anti-union. It's based on the idea that capital should be free to flow anywhere around the world in search of cheap labor. Countries are then forced to compete with each other over who can provide the most docile workers for the lowest wages and least benefits.

This competition has led to a deterioration in the purchasing power of the minimum wage. The real value of the minimum wage in Brazil fell 40 percent in the 1980s. Our minimum wage, which has cynically become the "maximum wage" for more than half the population, is a national disgrace. To say that $100 a month allows people to fulfill their basic needs, as the dominant sectors of Brazilian society claim, is an affront to human dignity. It also makes a mockery of the Constitution, which says that the minimum wage should provide workers and their families with their basic needs for housing, food, education, health, and transportation. I find it simply scandalous that big companies make enormous profits while their workers, the principal source of their wealth, don't even make subsistence wages.

There are a growing number of workers whose only alternative for housing is to sleep under bridges and on the streets, because the minimum wage they earn is not enough to pay for both food and rent. It's shameful how many people who live on the street are working people.

Of course, life is even worse for those who can't find any job at all. Unemployment is a major problem because our economic model doesn't generate nearly enough jobs for the growing population. In fact, unemployment is a growing problem all over the world. Workers are being laid off in record numbers, and new generations are finding there is no place for them in the workforce.

I can't stand it when I hear wealthy people say that people are poor because they are lazy and that if they only worked hard enough, they wouldn't be poor. The truth is that the ones who work the most in this country are the ones who earn the least. Like

many women, the work I did for so many years—cooking, cleaning, washing clothes, ironing—is not considered productive.
According to most economists, what counts is the capital accumulated by the big millionaires who often get rich by exploiting
cheap labor.

The globalization of the economy has brought about an intense
transformation of the entire world economic order. National
economies regulated by a sovereign state have been replaced by a
global economy with weak states. Brazil is perhaps the country in
Latin America that has most resisted the neoliberal model, and our
unions are on the forefront of this resistance. They are involved in
larger economic and political issues that have an impact on wage
policies and affect broad sectors of society.

When the Workers Party was formed in Brazil in the 1980s, a certain sector of the business community became quite nervous when
they saw that union organizers were not only talking about workplace issues but about national and international issues as well. The
unions started discussing issues like agrarian reform and the foreign
debt, issues that previously belonged to the closed world of bankers
and government economists. Since these issues have a direct influence on wage policies, it was essential for workers to get involved.

A strong union movement is critical to implementing policies
that favor workers. Even if only a relatively small portion of the
work force is unionized, many non-union employees benefit from
the gains of the unionized workers. Sometimes employers offer the
same wages—or even more—as a way to keep the unions out.
But the non-union workers often don't get other critical benefits,
such as guaranteed employment, health insurance, or pensions.

Look at a country like the United States, which is a wealthy,
powerful country but where the level of unionization—about 12
percent of the workforce—is abysmal. This is very alarming, con-
sidering that the only workers whose rights are protected are the
ones who have collective work contracts. Perhaps some highly spe-

cialized workers have individual contracts, but the majority are hired "at will." So only 12 percent of the workforce is protected against arbitrary dismissal and have legal rights to overtime, holidays, and other benefits, because a lot of these benefits are not established by law but by collective bargaining.

Many people in the United States think that it is inappropriate for unions to have formal ties to a political party. They are convinced that the role of the unions is exclusively to deal with workplace issues. Although the union federation AFL-CIO has a strong lobby in Washington and unions contribute to electoral campaigns, they don't have their own party or congress people who directly represent workers. But I think that unions should have formal party ties, for that is the only way that workers can have a say in determining policy.

In Brazil, despite severe repression, a progressive union federation called Central Única dos Trabalhadores, the Central Workers Union, was created in 1983. Today, it is the biggest union federation in the country, representing some 18 million workers—almost one-third of the work force. Thanks to the unions and the Workers Party, we managed to get a number of workers rights included in the Constitution, such as the legal right to paid holidays and time-and-a-half for overtime.

There are business people who insist that the legislation we passed in Brazil to protect workers' rights constricts foreign investment and makes it difficult to adapt labor relations to the new competitive conditions that Brazil faces. So they propose a series of changes to reduce the cost of labor. One is to eliminate the automatic adjustment of wages for inflation. Another is to allow people to collect social security only after they've reached a certain age, like 65, no matter how many years they've worked. This would particularly hurt poor people, since they start working at an early age and are presently able to collect their social security benefits after 30 years. Some business people also say we shouldn't force companies to pay for benefits like health care and social security. But I think that with today's savage capitalism, we need *more* protections for the work force, not less. The elimination or non-existence of fundamental workers' rights in many places around the world is leading to an alarming contradiction. At the same time that technical advances have reached heights never before imagined, we are witnessing the return of working conditions similar to the first decades of the industrial revolution, in which there were no limits on the workday and no workers' rights. In Brazil, these characteristics already exist in certain economic sectors, as in the coal mines, the shoe industry, and in certain sectors of agriculture.

Another factor that has been responsible for unemployment, loss of purchasing power, and increasing poverty in recent decades is the huge debt Brazil pays to foreign banks. Every year Brazil suffers from a hemorrhaging of resources that weakens and deforms our economy by consuming a major portion of our resources. These resources could be used for productive investments to benefit all Brazilians. Instead, they are transferred, in massive quantities, out of the country into the hands of international creditors.

During the two decades of the military dictatorship, billions of dollars in loans were acquired to develop huge infrastructure projects like road-building and dams. Millions of dollars in loans disappeared into the foreign bank accounts of corrupt officials, some projects were never even completed and there was no concern about the effects of these projects on the environment.

Under the military regime, the debt grew 40-fold. Today Brazil owes first world banks 120 billion dollars, the largest foreign debt in the third world, and we are paying about 10 billion dollars a year to service the debt. Adding insult to injury, if we look at how much we have reimbursed the banks so far in interest alone, the loans have already been paid several times over.

Despite the astronomical sums we've paid, the debt just keeps growing. Brazil is forced to take out new loans to pay the interest on past loans. Then these new loans increase the debt even more. So it's a vicious circle that has no end.

I get so angry when I think of how we could use the 10 billion dollars we pay the Western banks every year. It would be enough to build tens of thousands of health clinics or millions of low-income homes. It would allow us to implement social programs on a scale that would make a real difference in the lives of millions of poor Brazilians. Instead, to pay this debt we've had to slash social spending and throw even more people into destitution.

The debt and the reforms the international agencies like the World Bank and the International Monetary Fund force upon us to pay that debt have had disastrous consequences not only in Brazil but all over the world. Under the guise of monetary reform and humanitarian aid, these international agencies have taken much, much more capital out of the developed countries then they've invested. They've taken from the poor in the poor countries to pay the rich in the rich countries.

What we've witnessed in the past decades is that the rich nations have developed sophisticated mechanisms to control our countries without appearing as colonizing forces. Today, their arms of oppression and domination are not guns, but calculators. If we analyze our present circumstances and look back at history, we'll understand that what the people in the southern hemisphere are experiencing today is merely a more advanced and refined form of colonialism.

Thanks to our dependence on the international financial institutions, we've had to subordinate our economic policies to external decisions that run contrary to our national sovereignty. Our dependence allows these international institutions to tell our leaders what policies we can and can't implement.

We're not simply talking about a question of national sovereignty; we're talking about a question of life or death. The economic reforms we've been obligated to implement in recent years have led to a decline in life expectancy and an increase in infant mortality in dozens of countries. Sadly, these neocolonial policy prescriptions are responsible for eliminating critical social gains that had been won in previous decades with much struggle and sacrifice.

It's easy to see the results of this model when you look at Mexico, which was the first major victim of this neoliberal earthquake. Until the peso crash in 1995, the financial centers the world over were singing Mexico's praises. Mexico was the star pupil who carefully followed the dictates of the International Monetary Fund and was supposedly moving merrily along the much-celebrated road to modernity. But that road of opening up Mexico's economy to outside competition and slashing social programs to cut government spending led to an unprecedented level of misery during a time of economic growth. This disequilibrium provoked a social convulsion in the form of a guerrilla uprising in Chiapas and other parts of Mexico.

The peso crash brought down the whole house of cards, and it took billions of dollars in outside loans to keep the Mexican economy from totally collapsing. It will be especially difficult for Mexico to get out of this economic dependency now that it has signed the North American Free Trade Agreement with the United States and Canada. This agreement forces Mexico to accept the conditions imposed by international corporations. These same conditions are being imposed on all third world countries through other trade agreements such as the General Agreement on Tariffs and Trade, or GATT.

I remember in 1994 when the Brazilian Senate voted on the new text of GATT, which establishes the rules for world trade. We were asked for a straight up or down vote, without the right to question any of the provisions and with no public debate. It's a multilateral agreement that obliges member countries to give equal treatment to all their commercial trading partners, and not to put up barriers against imported products. My colleagues in the

Workers Party and I voted against it, but it passed anyway.

GATT is now being enforced by the World Trade Organization, which in the coming years will undoubtedly be a supranational force for controlling individual countries. It has unprecedented powers to impose penalties and other sanctions against member countries. And worst of all, its rulings are made behind closed doors by unelected representatives, and the public has no access to the decision-making process.

We certainly need international institutions to regulate issues that go beyond national boundaries, but not institutions that are controlled by big capital. There are other United Nations' agencies, like UNICEF, the World Health Organization, UNESCO and the International Labor Organization, that help improve social conditions in poor nations. But the UN is in a financial crisis, mostly because the big countries like the United States refuse to pay their allotted portion. Moreover, the major UN decisions are made by the five permanent members of the Security Council — the United States, Russia, China, England, and France — which have the power to veto any resolution.

This concentration of power in the hands of a few countries goes against the principle of equality between large and small nations that is in the preamble of the UN charter. The UN is made up of nearly 200 countries and to really be an effective place where all nations of the world can come together, it must be democratized. The decision-making body should be the General Assembly where all the nations are represented, not the Security Council.

Another way for southern countries to gain a better negotiating position vis-à-vis the north is to create more south-south links. The negotiations for the creation of a free market between Brazil, Argentina, Uruguay, and Paraguay, known as Mercosul, makes sense since these countries have similar economic conditions. However, there are still many issues to work out. The strong agricultural sector in Argentina can hurt farmers in the other countries; Brazil's more advanced industrial sector can make it hard for the other countries to compete. But at least we don't have the tremendous imbalances that exist between Mexico and the United States, imbalances that put Mexico in a subordinate position within NAFTA.

I think Mercosul could serve as model of cooperation between Third World countries if we can make sure that it doesn't benefit just the multinational corporations, becoming an instrument for companies to jump from one country to another in search of cheap labor. The inclusion of the social clause proposed by the unions would guarantee workers the freedom to organize, prohibit child labor, ensure health and safety regulations, and protect against discrimination in the workplace. If we can get this clause passed, then I would be more optimistic about having free trade agreements with our Latin neighbors.

I'd also like to see Brazil have closer commercial ties with Africa, and I've been fighting in the Commission on Foreign Relations to make this happen. I feel a great affinity with Africa because of historical and racial ties. After all, it was Africans who built Brazil. And with African countries like Mozambique and Angola, we share the bond of a common language and the common heritage of being colonized by Portugal.

Right now Africa accounts for only three percent of our foreign trade. But there is great potential in areas like agriculture, energy, and oil. Africa has important natural resources and Brazil has achieved an advanced level of technology in these areas, so greater collaboration could be of mutual benefit.

The new economic order demands global networks. If we don't form our own trading blocks, we will not be able to find solutions to issues like the foreign debt, protectionism, and economic dependence.

We also need to renegotiate the foreign debt. The first step is to reevaluate the debt—how it was acquired, how it became so massive, on what terms the loans were made, and how much has already been paid off. After the evaluation, we should establish new conditions to pay a fair share of the debt. We shouldn't have to bear the total responsibility for bad loans made to the corrupt military regime under onerous conditions. The Club of Paris, which represents private banks, recently cut Poland's debt in half, acknowledging that the new government should not be responsible for errors made by previous regimes. Why shouldn't other countries like Brazil warrant similar concessions?

We have to stop capital flight so that money made in Brazil is used to build up the country, not to buy condominiums in Florida. And we have to make the rich in Brazil pay their fair share of taxes. Right now, most Brazilian businesses and elites don't pay taxes. There is very weak enforcement of the law, and the rich find all sorts of ways to evade payments. According to government estimates, only half of all taxes owed to the government are ever collected, resulting in a loss of $80 billion a year. We need to tighten the loopholes so we can actually collect the taxes.

We need a development model that sees the generation of employment as an objective in and of itself. That's why I call for a strategy that focuses on micro, small and medium enterprises, because it's the small businesses that generate the most jobs, especially for workers who are not highly skilled.

Another way to generate employment is through land reform that would give the landless their own plots so they wouldn't have to migrate to the cities. A better distribution of land would also increase food production for domestic consumption, stimulating the internal market. Right now, we're one of the major agricultural exporters in the world but we don't produce food for our own people. In a country with 160 million people, we have to put more emphasis on our own internal market, a market that could generate so much production and so many jobs!

We have to stimulate the internal market and invest in products for everyday use. For example, Brazil produces clothing and shoes, but it's often cheaper to buy them outside Brazil. We have to make locally produced goods available at cheaper prices, and we have to combat the mentality that foreign goods are better than Brazilian ones.

The Workers Party has tried to introduce projects that could have great impact at the national level, but we have a hard time getting Congress to even vote on them. When we tried to introduce legislation for unemployment insurance, it was killed before it even got to the floor. Sometimes I spend a whole year working to get a bill before Congress. But when the government and its allies want something voted on, they call a special session of Congress and force us to make a decision on the spot. We call this *rolo compressor*—steamrollering. And then they turn around and say the Workers Party presents no concrete alternatives.

Another problem we face is that sometimes our projects are approved, but their implementation depends on the individual states to allocate budgets for them. And the process for approving the budget gets turned into a political dispute. This is happening right now to several projects I introduced in Rio. The money to finish a children's cardiology wing of a public hospital, to give land titles to descendants of black slaves, and to create infant-care facilities in women's prisons is being held up for political reasons.

I didn't expect milk and honey, but these partisan political games are draining. Why can't we work together to reach common goals? Look at what happened when the Workers Party controlled the capital, Brasília, and worked closely with the federal government to invest in education. There used to be hundreds of children hanging around the bus station begging. Now you don't see those kids on the street anymore because we built new schools for 26,000 children. If we could do that in Brasília, why can't we do that in the rest of the country?

Most of all, we have to believe in, and fight for, a different model of development. The neoliberals were jumping up and down after the fall of the Berlin Wall, as if capitalism was the greatest thing. But what has capitalism done for Brazil? It's true that capitalism has made us a major economic player in the global market. We have one of the largest economies in the world. We have a relatively well-developed industrial base and a large agricultural export sector. But 32 million Brazilians are hungry and 60 million live in poverty.

Economic development, on its own, doesn't decrease social inequalities. Political action, supported by social pressure, is needed to tie economic development to social justice. We must find ways to ensure that economic growth gets translated into health care, education, and better social services for poor communities. Without the eradication of absolute poverty, economic development will never fulfill its social function and we will never have a truly democratic society that guarantees equal opportunity to all.

Fortunately, there are still some people who are resisting the new global economic order. There are still some of us who insist that poverty and misery are not the inevitable consequences of human society. There are still some of us who are determined to find a model of development that is aimed at the 60 million Brazilians who are presently excluded from sharing the wealth. There are still some of us who insist that we stop waiting for the pie to grow, and get on with the job of cutting it up.

Chapter Ten

All the More Reason
to Keep on Dreaming

Photo by Jorge Nunes

*"I dream of building a society where happiness is our
normal state of being."*

"Chorei, não procurei esconder, todos viram. Sentiram pena de mim, não precisava. Ali onde eu chorei qualquer um chorava. Dar a volta por cima que eu dei, quero ver quem dava."

"I cried, I didn't try to hide it, everyone saw me. They felt sorry for me but they didn't have to. In the state I was in, anyone would have cried. I'd like to see who could turn things around the way I did."

Song by Noite Ilustrada

Music is very important in my life. I don't know the technical aspects of music, but I love to listen and to sing. I used to sing in the church choir and I worked with children's choirs.

It's very difficult to sing choir music. I'm always so impressed when I go to church and hear people singing. It's hard to express the feeling I get when I hear this music. I feel a great sense of peace and tranquillity. One day, I got so inspired that I decided to write some songs. The lyrics and the melody came to me as if someone were singing in my ear. I took a piece of paper and a pen and started to write. I'm not a good singer, so I decided to ask my friend Marcos Mendes, whom I've known since he was a child, to sing my songs. I helped him make a record and he included three of my songs on it.

I remember a funny story about Marcos. One day, I was invited to a conference at the Methodist Church and I was asked to bring a singer with me. So I invited Marcos to come along. Everybody was giving him strange looks because he is so small and skinny, and because he didn't open his mouth during the whole event. When he finally got up to sing, the entire group was astonished at the beautiful voice that came pouring out! People started to congratulate me, patting me on the back and saying "He's very good, sister Benedita." My friends later told me that they were sure this guy was going to really embarrass me because they couldn't imagine him holding a tune. But Marcos has music in his soul.

For me every style of music has its moment—I like classical

music and popular Brazilian music. I'm from the generation of the waltz and the tango, and I also identify with capoeira and samba. I like singers like Paulinho da Viola and Jorginho do Império who sing about daily life in the *favela*. I like the new Afro-Brazilian groups like *Cidade Negra,* and I also love jazz, especially Ella Fitzgerald, Louis Armstrong, and Dizzy Gillespie.

I like romantic, melodious music. When I'm feeling lonely, I put on a real heart-breaker like the song by Alcione *"Vai sentir falta de mim. . ."* — You're gonna miss me. I cry my heart out and then I feel much better.

Some songs are written just to create controversy, like that samba by Martinho da Vila that goes, *". . . só pra contrariar, eu não fiz amor com ela. . ."* — "just to piss her off, I didn't make love with her." There's another song by Martinho da Vila that created a big fuss. It said *"Mulher, você não passa de uma mulher"* —"Woman, you're nothing more than a woman." Many women, including me, were furious with him. When I complained, he laughed and said, "Well, what are you? Aren't you a woman?" He adores women and what he really wanted to say was that there are all kinds of women, women who are *dengosa, caprichosa, preguiçosa* —affectionate, capricious, lazy. With all of their differences, they are all simply women.

I think that Martinho da Vila is one of the greatest composers of popular Brazilian music. I adore that *negão*—that black brother. I felt honored when he composed a song for me, especially because my friend Lecy Brandão recorded it. I get choked up every time I hear it. It goes: *"Mulher brasileira que compra fiado e pechincha na feira/ mulher brasileira, cidadã brasileira. Ela é deputada, ela é delegada, prefeita e juíza/ uma grande mulher com um grande ideal é o que a gente precisa.*—"A Brazilian woman who buys on credit and bargains in the market; a Brazilian woman, a Brazilian citizen; She's a deputy, she's a sheriff, a mayor, and a judge; a great woman with great vision, that's what we need."

★ ★ ★

This music reflects my history. Growing up poor, black, and female, I know what it means to live at the margin of society. I know what it's like to be a second class citizen. I learned early in life that the "service entrance" was my point of entry. I learned that the place for women was the kitchen. And I rebelled against all of this. Today I'm proud to be a black woman from a poor family. My origins provide me with a reference point that I will never reject. And it gives me the passion I need to keep fighting.

But fighting for what? After nearly 30 years of military rule, Brazil now has an elected government and is seen by the rest of the world as a democratic nation. But in a country where millions go hungry and justice is on the side of the rich, we have to question what democracy really means.

For me, democracy has many components. It means freedom to express your thoughts. It means freedom to practice your own religion. It means respect for racial and cultural differences. On the political front, democracy means the right to elect your own representatives, regardless of their race, sex, religion or class. It means one person, one vote, and the freedom to vote for whomever you want.

Most people would agree with these elements of democracy. But they leave out another dimension that is equally critical. When we talk about democracy, we have to incorporate rights like the right to a job at a decent wage, the right to a clean environment and the right to a more equitable form of development. These issues are as much a part of democracy as the right to free speech and free elections.

In Brazil, millions are denied their economic rights, and real power lies in the hands of a small minority. Decisions are made at the top, without the effective participation of the majority. And in this era of globalization, decisions by banks located thousands of miles away often have more impact on the daily lives of Brazilians than our own representatives do.

Many people equate capitalism and democracy, but so many of the capitalist countries I've visited have a false, unrepresentative democracy. Elections are bought and sold, economic power is concentrated in the hands of the few, and the media, which is controlled by the elite, has the power to distort the facts and confuse the public. I also see how capitalism distorts human values. In capitalist societies, people usually aspire to wealth and power instead of compassionate social relations.

That's why I believe we need something radically different. We need to transform our society into one where human relations take precedence over material things. Socialism, in theory, could do that. Unfortunately, it has been distorted in almost all the places it has been tried. But I think we must keep on trying, since the poorer countries of the world are in desperate need of new social experiments. I think we need to try a version of socialism that is not imported or top-down, but a kind of socialism that respects our culture and works from the bottom-up.

I don't advocate radical political change because I read about socialism in a book, but because of all the hardships I've been through and the difficulties I still confront in my personal life. Right now I'm dealing with the tragedy of my sister Dinha, who has cancer and has to rely on public hospitals for treatment. I feel desperate when I visit her and see the terrible conditions of our health care system. I can't believe that my sister worked so hard all her life, and now she can't even die with dignity. I know many people go through the same kind of trauma when they don't have money for decent health care, and this makes me even more depressed.

Yesterday, I was walking on the street thinking about my sister. I was feeling so depressed, and two teenagers who recognized me came up to chat. They wanted to know what I thought about the political climate and the results of our local elections. I was so sad that I really didn't feel like talking; I just wanted to cry. But when I looked at their beautiful, eager faces, I told myself: "Be strong. Hang in there, Bené!" I can't let down the people who identify with me and put great hope in me, the people who see me on the street and say things like: "Look, here is *our* senator!" or "We're so proud because you are just like us."

Of course, I also get people who feel that I've let them down. They thought that once I got into Congress, I should have been able to change the whole system. They ask, "Why aren't you doing anything for us in Congress? Have you forgotten about the unemployed, the elderly?" It's hard to hear those kinds of criticisms from my own constituents, but I also understand that most people have no idea what happens in Brasília because the information they get from the commercial media is very limited.

I haven't lost my idealism—I couldn't continue in politics without it—but I must admit that I'm not as much of an idealist as I used to be. I would find the political process a lot more enticing if our political battles weren't so destructive. I wish we could have a political process where we didn't destroy, discredit, invalidate or annihilate each other. Before I got into politics, I'd heard it said that some people would go to any length to get power. Now I've seen the back-room dealings from up close, but I'm still shocked at how dirty and degrading they can get.

I dream of a different kind of society, a society where communities come together and organize themselves, and the government is forced to take their lead. I dream of a society that not only guarantees all Brazilians a job, food, and a roof over their heads, but an opportunity to relax and enjoy life, an opportunity to be happy.

I know that happiness can't be a permanent state. Human beings are constantly changing and we have our moments of frustration, sadness, depression. But I also don't think of happiness as a carnival, where you work all year long to have your moment of fantasy and then you go back to the same old daily grind. We should try to build a society where happiness is our normal state of being.

For me, ideology is not the key issue. Whether you believe in capitalism or socialism as the best social system is really irrelevant.

The most important thing is what you do in your everyday life to make the world better. The most important thing is your actions. You may believe that in theory, people shouldn't go hungry, but if you don't do anything to stop hunger, then your thoughts are meaningless. I've already been hungry, so it's not just an intellectual exercise for me. It's a question of doing something so that others don't have to suffer like I did.

In the 1960's, people dreamed the impossible. After all, the world context was propitious to thinking big. It was a time of euphoria when the students were taking to the streets of Paris demanding fraternity and equality. It was the time of the Prague Spring when there were hopes of political reform in the Eastern bloc. It was the time of the Watts uprising in Los Angeles that reshaped the civil rights laws in the United States. It was the time of the student struggles in Mexico that were violently crushed by the Tlatelolco massacre. It was the time of the worldwide movement against the war in Vietnam.

"Never say never" was the cry of those times. People the world over were fighting for freedom. The order of the day was to break down barriers, to challenge prejudices, to give a voice to the voiceless, the forgotten, the oppressed.

In some ways, we've lost that sense of euphoria, that sense of making the impossible possible. The ensuing years have been difficult ones, with wages and living conditions declining all over the world. We still see courageous forms of resistance, but today it's more difficult to envision radical change. Somehow, we have to regain the momentum. Somehow, we have to be able to dream again.

I want to see more working people and poor people in power. I want to see the PT win the presidency. I want to see respect for children's rights, a better distribution of wealth, and jobs for all. I want to see the business community take pride in building a more equitable economic system. I want to see a society that does not separate rich and poor, black and white, men and women.

Does the society I envision already exist anywhere in the world? Not really. But that's all the more reason to keep on dreaming. And I know that while I'm here dreaming in Chapéu Mangueira, one of the many *favelas* in Rio, I am joined by people from Harlem to Soweto to Chiapas who have the same vision. No matter our race, nationality or religion, we are brothers and sisters if we are united by the same longing for justice.

But to transform those dreams into reality, we all need to recognize our responsibility to take action. This action can take a thousand different forms—from finding housing for the homeless to stopping domestic violence to advocating for global disarmament.

I know in my own work how easy it is to feel overwhelmed by the vastness of the problems, to feel completely insignificant and defeated. It's precisely in those moments of self-doubt that we have to pull ourselves up and find our inner strength. We have to seek the embrace of our family, our friends, our community. And we need to understand that we are part of a larger struggle that reaches way beyond particular issues or national boundaries.

In my lifetime I have had the privilege of meeting thousands of inspiring women from around the world, like during the Women's Conference in China, and meeting extraordinary individuals like Nelson Mandela and Jesse Jackson. These opportunities have allowed me to see the interconnectedness and the global dimensions of our work. They have given me a tremendous sense of pride to be part of this movement—a movement that values the sanctity of human life more than material possessions, and places human need over human greed. I hope that each one of you feels somehow connected to this life-affirming struggle. And I hope that you, too, take pride in being in the company of such remarkable brothers and sisters.

Caribbean Sea

North Atlantic Ocean

VENEZUELA

GUYANA

SURINAME

FRENCH GUIANA (FRANCE)

COLOMBIA

ECUADOR

PERU

BRAZIL

BRASILIA

South Pacific Ocean

BOLIVIA

CHILE

PARAGUAY

RIO DE JANEIRO

ARGENTINA

URUGUAY

South Atlantic Ocean

FALKLAND ISLANDS (U.K.)

SOUTH GEORGIA ISLAND (U.K.)

Key Political Events in Brazil During Benedita da Silva's Life

1930-45—Getúlio Vargas became president for the first time. Benedita was born toward the end of his regime in March of 1943. After a brief interlude (1946-50), Vargas was elected again. Facing increasing opposition, he was ousted on August 24, 1954, and committed suicide the same day.

1955—Juscelino Kubitschek was elected president. In 1960 he moved the capital from Rio de Janeiro to Brasília with the purpose of developing the interior of the country.

1960—Two divergent politicians were elected for president and vice president: Jânio Quadros of the National Democratic Union which was Brazil's largest conservative party at the time, and João Goulart of the Brazilian Labor Party. After seven months, President Jânio Quadros resigned and Vice President João Goulart assumed office.

1964—Goulart was ousted by a military coup. On April 11, General Castelo Branco took power. He eliminated all existing political parties until 1966, when a two-party system was created. The new political parties were the government's National Renewal Alliance (ARENA) and the opposition party called the Brazilian Democratic Movement (MDB).

1967—Castelo Branco created a new constitution, expanding the power of the military and establishing indirect presidential elections.

1968—General Costa e Silva was chosen president by Congress. Repression against the opposition worsened, with hundreds of people being arrested, tortured, killed and exiled. Costa e Silva suffered a stroke in 1969, when General Emilio Médici was chosen to be president.

1974—General Ernesto Geisel was elected president by an electoral college and the opposition party, MDB, greatly increased its number of representatives in Congress. In 1977, President Geisel dismissed Congress for blocking the judicial reforms he had proposed.

1979—Geisel's successor, General João Batista Figueiredo, enacted a general amnesty, restoring political rights to those who had been in prison or exiled. In the 1980s, Brazil developed a significant industrial complex. At the same time, it acquired the largest foreign debt in the Third World, creating a great economic gap between the rich and the poor.

Massive general strikes by metal workers in São Paulo were severely repressed by the government. The workers began organizing a new political party, the Workers Party, with support from popular movements such as Benedita's neighborhood association.

1982—First direct elections for city and state government in which the Workers Party participated. Benedita da Silva was elected to Rio's City Council.

1985—In an indirect election, MDB candidate, Tancredo Neves, was selected for the presidency. He died shortly before his inauguration, and Vice President José Sarney took power. In 1986, Benedita was elected to Congress and participated in the creation of a new constitution. This period marked the transition to democracy.

1988—The new constitution was promulgated, eliminating government censorship and establishing political and social freedoms. It provided for a presidential election in 1989, when Fernando Collor de Mello of the National Reconstruction Party won 43 percent of the votes, and Luiz Inácio Lula da Silva of the Workers Party received 38 percent of the votes in the final round. Benedita was reelected to Congress in 1990.

1992—President Fernando Collor de Mello resigned under accusations of corruption, shortly before the final vote by Congress on his impeachment trial. Vice President Itamar Franco assumed the presidency. Benedita ran for mayor of Rio de Janeiro, losing by a three percent margin.

1994—In the presidential election, Worker Party leader Luiz Inácio Lula da Silva led in the polls by 20 percent until two months before the vote, but lost after the government launched an emergency economic plan to stop inflation. Fernando Henrique Cardoso of the Brazilian Social Democratic Party was elected president, and began implementing structural adjustment policies, including the privatization of national industries. Benedita da Silva was elected to the Senate.

Suggested Readings

Alvarez, Sonia. *Engendering Democracy in Brazil.* Princeton, NJ: Princeton University Press, 1990.

Branford, Sue, and Bernardo Kucinski. *Brazil, Carnival of the Oppressed: Lula and the Brazilian Workers Party.* New York: Monthly Review Press, 1996.

Capoeira Women's Group. *Women in Brazil.* New York: Monthly Review Press, 1996.

Chalmers, Douglas, ed. *The New Politics of Inequality in Latin America.* New York: Oxford University Press, 1997.

Dalla Costa, Mariarosa and Giovanna Dalla Costa. *Paying the Price: Women and the Politics of International Economic Strategy.* Milano, Italy: Franco Angeli, 1993.

Danaher, Kevin and Michael Shellenberger, eds. *Fighting for the Soul of Brazil.* New York: Monthly Review Press, 1995.

Dimenstein, Gilberto. *Brazil: War on Children.* New York: Monthly Review Press, 1996.

Gross, Tony. *Fight for the Forest: Chico Mendes in His Own Words.* New York: Monthly Review Press, 1996.

Jaquette, Jane S. *The Women's Movement in Latin America.* Denver: Westview Press, 1994.

Page, Joseph. *The Brazilians.* Reading, MA: Addison-Wesley Publishing Co., 1995.

Patai, Daphne. *Brazilian Women Speak: Contemporary Life Stories.* New Brunswick, NJ: Rutgers University Press, London, 1993.

Rocha, Jan. *Brazil in Focus.* New York: Interlink, 1996.

Sader, Emir, and Ken Silverstein. *Without Fear of Being Happy: Lula, the Worker's Party, and Brazil.* New York: Verso Press, 1991.

About Benedita

BENEDITA DA SILVA, who was born on March 11, 1943, grew up in the *favelas* (shantytowns) of Rio in a family of thirteen siblings. She led a life of excruciating poverty. She watched two of her four children die of curable diseases, barely survived a back alley abortion, and was exploited and humiliated as a live-in maid.

But Benedita is a fighter. She organized her neighbors in the *favela* to get water, sewers and electricity. She learned to read and write, and then taught other women. In 1982, she took the extraordinary step of running for political office in Rio as a Workers Party candidate, becoming the nation's first black city councilwoman. In 1986, she became a Federal Deputy and is now a Senator. She has fought the foreboding obstacles of race, gender and poverty with creativity and charm. And, as she herself says, she has emerged a champion.

Bené, as she is known, has not forgotten her roots. She still lives in the Chapéu Mangueira favela in Rio, although she flies back and forth to the nation's capital, Brasília, every week. She dedicates her political life to advocating for a better life for those who are marginalized and oppressed, especially women, blacks, street children, and indigenous people.

About the Authors

MEDEA BENJAMIN is co-founder and co-director of the human rights group Global Exchange, and lectures widely on issues of human rights and corporate responsibility. Her books include *Bridging the Global Gap: A Handbook to Linking Citizens of the First and Third Worlds* (Seven Locks Press, 1989); *Don't be Afraid Gringo: A Honduran Woman Speaks from the Heart* (Harper Collins, 1987); *No Free Lunch: Food and Revolution in Cuba Today* (Grove Press, 1986) and *The Peace Corps and More: 175 ways to Work Study and Travel at Home and Abroad* (Global Exchange, 1997). She worked for the United Nations' Food and Agriculture Organization in Africa and Latin America, and was a senior analyst with the Institute for Food and Development Policy (Food First). Ms. Benjamin received a Masters in economics from the New School for Social Research and a Masters in public health from Columbia University.

MARIA LUISA (MAISA) MENDONÇA is coordinator of the Brazil Program at Global Exchange. She is a videographer whose documentary work has been presented on television and in festivals in the U.S., Canada, Europe and Latin America. In 1992 she received an award by the Banff Center for the Arts for her experimental video *Contact and Contrast,* and in 1995 she was awarded by the Film Arts Foundation for her documentary *Instants* about a Chilean immigrant family in the U.S. In 1994 she produced *Everyday Art,* a tribute to Cuban traditional music and dance, and in 1996 she produced *Islands on Fire,* a documentary exposing human rights abuses in Indonesia and East Timor. Ms. Mendonça received a M.A. degree in Broadcast and Electronic Communications from San Francisco State University.

G L O B A L E x c h a n g e

Global Exchange is a human rights organization that work in the following areas:

• **Reality Tours:** We provide participants with a *feel* for the people of a country. We meet with farmers, human rights and peace activists, church workers, environmentalists, government officials and opposition leaders. We visit countries such as Cuba, Mexico, Haiti, South Africa, Ireland, Brazil and Vietnam. We also feature California tours investigating issues such as immigration, chemical vs. organic agriculture, and the struggle over the ancient redwoods.

• **Public Education:** Global Exchange publishes books and pamphlets on a wide range of issues: world hunger, free trade vs. fair trade, the IMF & World Bank, Mexico, Cuba, Brazil and many other issues. We also make regular radio appearances, and organize conferences and workshops. Our Speakers Bureau provides colleges and community groups with inspiring speakers on subjects such as globalization, the United Nations, how to work in the Third World, the world food system and U.S. farming, and U.S. Foreign Policy.

• **Fair Trade:** To help build economic justice from the ground up, Global Exchange promotes alternative trade that benefits low-income producers and artisan co-ops. Sales at our Berkeley and San Francisco fair trade stores support thousands of craftspeople in more than 30 developing countries and help educate people here in the U.S. about foreign cultures and international trade.

• **Human Rights** Work: By putting outside eyes and ears into conflict situations, Global Exchange helps report on and restrain repressive government forces. We arrange election observation teams, produce human rights reports and bring long-term volunteers into conflict zones such as the southern Mexican state of Chiapas.

• **Material Assistance:** Global Exchange provides money and technical support to successful grassroots groups in Mexico, Cuba, Vietnam, Cambodia, South Africa, the United States and other countries. Our assistance has ranged from supporting a peasant-run literacy program in Honduras to providing scholarships for poor rural girls in Vietnam who would otherwise not be able to continue their education.

Global Exchange works to create more justice and economic opportunity in the world. The heart of our work is the involvement of thousands of supporters around the country.

When you become a member of Global Exchange you get:

- our quarterly newsletter and Action Alerts;
- priority on our Reality Tours to dozens of foreign countries and domestic destinations;
- a 10 percent discount on our educational materials and the crafts we sell at our third world craft stores;
- regular updates on our material aid campaigns and our support for development projects;

Plus, you get connected to a growing international network of concerned citizens working to transform the world from the bottom up.

Please use the form below to join Global Exchange today.

YES, I support Global Exchange's efforts to reform the global economy. Here is my tax-deductible membership donation:

_____ $100 _____ $50 _____ $35 _____ $25

Name _____

Address _____

City _____ State _____ Zip _____

Phone_____

G L O B A L 🌐 E X C H A N G E

2017 Mission Street, Suite 303, San Francisco, CA 94110
(415) 255-7296, FAX (415) 255-7498
gx-info@globalexchange.org
website: www.globalexchange.org

More Books from Food First

The Future in the Balance: Essays on Globalization and Resistance
Walden Bello
Edited with a preface by Anuradha Mittal
   A new collection of essays by Third World activist and scholar Walden Bello on the myths of development as prescribed by the World Trade Organization and other institutions, and the possibility of another world based on fairness and justice.   Paperback, $13.95   ISBN: 0-935028-84-6

Views from the South: The Effects of Globalization
and the WTO on Third World Countries
Foreword by Jerry Mander
Afterword by Anuradha Mittal
Edited by Sarah Anderson
   This rare collection of essays by Third World activists and scholars describes in pointed detail the effects of the WTO and other Bretton Woods institutions.   Paperback, $12.95   ISBN: 0-935028-82-x

Basta! Land and the Zapatista Rebellion in Chiapas
Revised edition
George A. Collier with Elizabeth Lowery Quaratiello
Foreword by Peter Rosset
   The classic on the Zapatistas in a new revised edition, including a preface by Roldolfo Stavenhagen, a new epilogue about the present challenges to the indigenous movement in Chiapas, and an updated bibliography.   Paperback, $14.95   ISBN: 0-935028-79-x

America Needs Human Rights
Edited by Anuradha Mittal and Peter Rosset
   This new anthology includes writings on understanding human rights, poverty in America, and welfare reform and human rights.
   Paperback, $13.95   ISBN: 0-935028-72-2

The Paradox of Plenty: Hunger in a Bountiful World
Edited by Douglas H. Boucher
   Excerpts from Food First's best writings on world hunger and what we can do to change it.   Paperback, $18.95   ISBN: 0-935028-71-4

A Siamese Tragedy: Development and Disintegration in Modern Thailand
Walden Bello, Shea Cunningham, and Li Kheng Poh
Critiques the failing economic system that has propelled the Thai people down an unstable path.
Paperback, $19.95   ISBN: 0-935028-74-9

Dark Victory: The United States and Global Poverty
Walden Bello, with Shea Cunningham and Bill Rau
Second edition, with a new epilogue by the author
Offers an understanding of why poverty has deepened in many countries, and analyzes the impact of US economic policies.
Paperback, $14.95   ISBN: 0-935028-61-7

Education for Action: Undergraduate and Graduate Programs
That Focus on Social Change
Fourth edition
Edited by Joan Powell
A newly updated authoritative and easy-to-use guidebook that provides information on progressive programs in a wide variety of field.
Paperback, $12.95   ISBN: 0-935028-86-2

Alternatives to the Peace Corps:
Third World and US Volunteer Opportunities
Ninth edition
Edited by Joan Powell
Over one hundred listings of organizations in the United States and the Third World provide the prospective volunteer an array of choices to make their commitment count.
Paperback, $9.95   ISBN: 0-935028-83-8

Call our distributor to place book orders.

CDS
(800) 343-4499

JOINING FOOD FIRST

☐ I want to join Food First and receive a 20% discount
on this and all subsequent orders. Enclosed
is my tax-deductible contribution of:

☐ $100   ☐ $50   ☐ $35

NAME _____

ADDRESS _____

CITY/STATE/ZIP _____

DAYTIME PHONE (_____) _____

E-MAIL _____

ORDERING FOOD FIRST MATERIALS

ITEM DESCRIPTION	QTY	UNIT COST	TOTAL

PAYMENT METHOD:

☐ CHECK

☐ MONEY ORDER

☐ MASTERCARD

☐ VISA

MEMBER DISCOUNT, 20% $ _____

CA RESIDENTS SALES TAX 8.25% $ _____

SUBTOTAL $ _____

POSTAGE: 15%   UPS: 20%   ($2 MIN.) $ _____

MEMBERSHIP(S) $ _____

ADDITIONAL CONTRIBUTION $ _____

TOTAL ENCLOSED $ _____

NAME ON CARD _____

CARD NUMBER _____ EXP. DATE _____

SIGNATURE _____

MAKE CHECK OR MONEY ORDER PAYABLE TO:

Food First, 398 - 60th Street, Oakland, CA 94618